"An amazing story of a determined young woman who went from the streets to the stage for the glory of God. Knowing Jeannie since she first came to Metro Sunday school in Brooklyn as a young girl, I knew the odds had been stacked against her from day one. It is no secret what God can do in the life of someone who is willing to turn theirs over to Him."

Bill Wilson, pastor and founder, Metro World Child

"What a read! Jeannie has written *What Is Happening to Me?* with a fierce passion that will inspire, encourage and catapult you right out of anything that may be holding you back or harnessing you to defeat! You won't be able to put this book down! I greatly appreciate her candid life transparency that paints a pathway to hope and victory!"

Dr. Tracy Strawberry, author; speaker;
founder, Finding Your Way

"My dear friend Jeannie Ortega Law's book *What Is Happening to Me?* is an honest and eye-opening spiritual coming-of-age account of her growing up in New York City. She shares how the God of the universe intersected her life of self-doubt, confusion and fear and enabled her to break free and conquer her childhood traumas and spiritual deviancy. This book is a practical, step-by-step guide to understanding the power, authority and love of God, which can free us to experience the new identity we have in Christ! If you're confused about your faith in God, pick up this book and find the clarity you've been looking for!"

Joe Battaglia, author; founder, Renaissance
Communications; co–executive producer, *Keep the Faith*

"Jeannie Ortega Law has faced the work of Satan like few have. She faced it as a young child, she faced it growing up, and she knows how to overcome the devil. I recommend this book to anyone who truly wants to be free from Satan's power."

Bishop Tom Brown, founder and pastor,
Word of Life Church, El Paso, Texas

"Jeannie captivates us right from the first sentence with her transparency, evoking truth and informing us that we must be aware of the spiritual battle we encounter here on earth. She packs the pages full of powerful Scripture to utilize as we do battle against an enemy we can't see. *What Is Happening To Me?* reminds us that every life is beautiful, ordained by God and powered by the Holy Spirit. The book is a must read for such a time as this!"

Shari Rigby, actress, *Overcomer* and *October Baby*;
author, *Consider the Lilies* and *Beautifully Flawed*;
motivational speaker

WHAT IS HAPPENING TO ME?

WHAT IS HAPPENING TO ME?

HOW TO DEFEAT YOUR UNSEEN ENEMY

JEANNIE ORTEGA LAW

Chosen

a division of Baker Publishing Group
Minneapolis, Minnesota

Library of Congress Cataloging-in-Publication Data
Names: Ortega Law, Jeannie, author.
Title: What is happening to me?: how to defeat your unseen enemy / Jeannie Ortega Law.
Description: Minneapolis, Minnesota: Chosen Books, [2021]
Identifiers: LCCN 2020037977 | ISBN 9780800761769 (trade paperback) | ISBN 9780800762285 (casebound) | ISBN 9781493430147 (ebook)
Subjects: LCSH: Spiritual warfare. | Discernment (Christian theology) | Spiritual exercises.
Classification: LCC BV4509.5 .O795 2021 | DDC 235/.4—dc23
LC record available at https://lccn.loc.gov/2020037977

CONTENTS

FOREWORD

I met Jeannie in 2012 when she appeared on a TBN broadcast my wife, Tracy, and I were hosting. We were first blessed by her anointed music and then the testimony of what God had done in her life.

Like Jeannie, my home life drove me to pursue fame. But I did not see what the enemy was doing. Soon I was led astray down a dark path. Neither of us knew we were under the attack of the enemy, whose goal is to steal, kill and destroy God's purpose. But God's grace and mercy snatched us out of the darkness. Now as followers of Christ we know the tricks of the enemy, so we can defeat him and overcome.

I have a heart for people, especially those who are faced with conditions, situations or battles in their lives that bring a deep sense of hopelessness to the soul. It is hard to see what is happening on the inside or in the spiritual realm. Rejection, abuse and brokenness in my life led to some really bad habits. I was successful by the world's standards but broken. At my lowest point, I was diagnosed with colon cancer, and was a liar, cheater, womanizer, alcoholic and drug addict. But God pulled me out of a pit and saved me.

When you have as many troubles as I did, it is easy to want to give up. When you want to give up on yourself, and when others may be finished with you, God is never, ever finished with you. He meets you where you are at.

We do not always know what is going on in our lives. But God has put this book into your life to help. Whatever your starting point, God will help you get out of your pit and onto a solid rock. The devil is always going to be busy. Do not miss the miracle of God in your life by giving up too soon. Do not quit, no matter what. Jesus is here to rescue you, redeem you with His blood and restore you with His grace.

Jeannie is having a powerful impact on her generation, and her message is for anyone who believes God is still in the business of turning lives around. Nothing is greater than finding Jesus and discovering His purpose for your life. Although I came to know Jesus in 1991, I was not discipled to walk with Him. I had worldly knowledge but not Kingdom knowledge, and you only get Kingdom knowledge when you pick up the Word of God and put it into practice in your life. This book will help disciple you from wherever you are into a place of freedom.

I trust that as you read your eyes will be opened. God has called you to great things. Taste and see that God is good. He is better than anything you could hope for.

Darryl Strawberry
Four-time World Series Champion,
author, speaker and founder of Strawberry Ministries

1

How Lies Begin

t is not fair to pick on a child, but the enemy of your soul does it all the time. The evil one begins telling you lies before you can even comprehend what a lie is. In turn, these lies shape your world and everything you believe and know to be reality. I have learned that what you cannot see can actually hurt you. In this book, I hope to help you learn how to discern what is happening in the spiritual realm. As a result, you will be able to overcome anything that is not of God. God sees beyond the distortion of this world, and He wants us to be able to as well. He desires that we walk in our God-given inheritance as His born-again children who walk in the Spirit.

Let me begin by sharing with you what the enemy did to get the lies started in my life. In doing so, I pray that my story will help you recognize the evil devices he is trying to employ in your life.

The Probability of Me

I almost died before I was born. I am an eighties baby who was conceived during an era when getting rid of a baby in the womb was not encouraged, as it is today. My parents were in their mid and late twenties, and a whole mess of things had led them to each other. They had been married four years when they found out they were pregnant with me. At this season of their lives, they were still learning how to survive marriage and create a unified team. My mother often tells me that if she had known having kids would have made her marriage better, she would have done it a lot sooner.

It was not until I asked her recently to tell me everything about that period in her life that she revealed to me that having me was something that she and my dad chose to do. They had an abortion before my birth, and they had one after I was born. My birth was allowed intentionally to happen. To this day she can barely speak about it. I asked her to share her story with me so that I could communicate it accurately. It was important for me to know the whole truth.

Before I was born, I was pursued by the threat of death. You might have heard the Scripture "The thief comes only to steal and kill and destroy" (John 10:10). He often starts early. I cannot imagine a better way to take out a generation of world changers who are created in the image of God than to persuade their parents that life only begins outside of the womb. If that is a lie they believe, then they can choose to end that life before it ever begins. My mom and dad had their reasons for what they chose at the time—as do others who make similar decisions—but I am grateful that by God's grace I made it to the other side.

God urges us to choose life. "Today I have given you the choice between life and death, between blessings and curses. Now I call on heaven and earth to witness the choice you make. Oh, that you would choose life, so that you and your descendants might live" (Deuteronomy 30:19 NLT). I believe He equips us to do what the enemy sometimes tries to convince us that we cannot do.

Right up until the moment of my birth my parents believed I was a boy. That belief came from a few things. First, doctors did not conduct sonograms at that time—at least not in my mother's neighborhood. Second, I was born into a superstitious family. My mother's family practiced a religion that believed spirits communicated with them, and those "spirits" said that I would be a boy. My dad already had two girls and one boy from his first marriage, so I think they wanted another boy to even things out.

I find it fascinating how people are always looking to structure things so that their lives can function smoothly. The heavenly realm functions within a similar system of structure. Perhaps that is why the human race is bent toward following that pattern. In my studies of the spiritual realm, I have learned that there is the mystery of the Godhead—who is three in one, Father, Spirit and Son—but that there are also other spiritual beings.

The evil one goes by many names: Satan, devil, adversary, accuser, tempter or serpent. He does not want to live under God's authority. We learn of this evil creature in the beginning of the Bible in Genesis 3. When we meet him, he is in the Garden of Eden tempting Adam and Eve to sin. He is our first illustration of evil. He distorts truth and tries tirelessly to drag God's creation into spiritual rebellion.

This being is against everything that is good, and he works through lies to lead humanity into disorder. These forces of both good and evil had an impact on my life from the very beginning.

My Abrupt Entrance

I guess I have never been one to be subtle in anything, and I came into this world in a similar fashion. My mom's due date was December of 1986, but she recalls that timeline changing after she was given a plant from one of her superstitious relatives. The Rose of Jericho, also known as the Resurrection Plant, is commonly found in northern Africa and southwest Asia. Despite starting as a shriveled brown ball, it will transform itself into a vibrant plant with brilliant green leaves. This transformation is what people believe gives it its mystical qualities.

It is said by those who practice magic that a house where the Rose of Jericho is kept is a blessed house. My mom was given the plant as a gift during her pregnancy with me. Shortly after receiving the plant, approximately a month before I was supposed to be born, my mother walked into the room where she kept the obscure plant and it bloomed right before her eyes. Moments later her water broke, and she was rushed to the hospital for an early delivery. Coincidence? It was not considered as such in our superstitious family. Even now as a Christian, I believe it could have been a spiritual indication that there was about to be a war in the heavenlies for my entrance into this world.

I asked my mom recently if she believed the plant was a sign from God, or if she thought it was some evil sign of a threat against my life. She told me that even if it was an attack on my life the enemy lost, because I am here and am a blessing to many. Her positive perspective is right. We should always be grateful for the victory after the battle rather than focusing on the battle itself. Paul speaks about this in the book of Colossians. He says, "Don't let anyone capture you with empty philosophies and high-sounding nonsense that come from human thinking and from the spiritual powers of this world, rather than from Christ" (Colossians 2:8 NLT).

Some people love stories that are steeped in superstition, but my very pregnant mom was afraid for both of our lives. She went into labor as I was in a breech position and premature. Because complications were a possibility, my mother had to go into emergency surgery and have me via C-section. In the eighties this procedure was risky for both the mom and baby. By the grace of God, I made it. The only indicators that the process had been tenuous was that I received a black eye and had a stint in an incubator. All things considered, we both made it out alive and well.

Every human is born into a state of war whether or not they realize it, like it or want it. The spiritual realm is battling for them until the end of their lives, and it does not abandon the mission. Looking back on your life, have you ever felt the threat? Would you say you were oblivious to it because you were not aware? Maybe a threat was disguised as something you now accept as normal. I believe an enemy placed a target on my back before I entered the earth. What was very evident was that it never had true power over my destiny. Having said that, it does not mean that the evil spiritual forces ever gave up trying to thwart my purpose.

Dealing with Envy

Once we were allowed to go home from the hospital, my little life soon became exposed to another great evil that infects the people of this world: envy. I was one of the few in my family who was born with green eyes. This was a recessive trait that was passed down from my father's mother. Neither my parents nor my siblings had this eye color, so I stuck out like a sore thumb. As life went on, I got to see the spirit of envy rear its ugly head many times. For the sake of amusing myself, I called it Cousin Envy.

At this stage of my life I do not always see it, but it comes around from time to time. This is true especially when life is going well. Envy is always looking to leech off of me. Getting distracted by envy has drained the joy out of many blessings. It is something to keep an eye out for.

Throughout the book of Psalms, every time we see the word *blessed* it is defined as, "happy, fortunate, and to be envied." If you are like me and being envied is something you have dealt with in your life, you should recognize that it is an attack from the enemy of your soul. His intention is to hinder your life. Do not fret. Look at it as the Bible does. You are blessed! "Happy and blessed are the people who are in such a case; yes, happy (blessed, fortunate, prosperous, to be envied) are the people whose God is the Lord!" (Psalm 144:15 AMPC).

My parents describe me as having been a friendly and brave little baby. I would hop out of my carriage while it was in motion, and I would jump down steps and off of furniture. Apparently, I made friends with everyone. My mom said I became the family and neighborhood star, which, of course, did not help the case of others being envious of me. They said my personality led to what Latinx people call *mal de ojo* or "evil eye." The evil eye is said to be a curse brought on by excessive admiration or a malevolent glare.

In my Puerto Rican culture, infants are considered to be very susceptible to the evil eye because of their innocence. I was given a special bracelet called *Manita de Azabache*, which is a gold bracelet with a dark hand hanging from it. This symbol is meant to ward off evil and should never be removed. "For where jealousy and selfish ambition exist, there will be disorder and every vile practice" (James 3:16). This verse followed me into adulthood.

My parents must have felt the envy over me, because they did what they knew to do at the time to keep me safe. My mother's best friend christened me in the Catholic Church. This was a tradition that my Catholic family deemed necessary for every infant. They believed it was a way to ensure that a covenant was made between a child and God. Even though my parents and godparents vowed to raise me in the statutes of God, my mom confessed that her real focus was on the lack of peace at home. She described those days as a war zone due to the violence that surrounded her.

As an adult, I was rebaptized. I felt it was important to do when I could comprehend fully what baptism signified. Jesus was an adult when He was baptized. As John the Baptist said, he baptized people for repentance (see Matthew 3:11). I wanted to understand all of that and be immersed in the water as a symbol of my faith, too.

My infant baptism was filled with strife, and evil was all around. In contrast, as an adult I was dunked in a pool and immediately saw heaven open up. I saw angels all around me. It was truly glorious. I believe that the glimpse into the spiritual realm that I received was God's way of solidifying that there is more around us than the eye can see.

It would be a long time before I would see that type of glory and feel the peace that comes with that outward profession of faith on a regular basis. I believe, however, that because of these early spiritual practices, God had a stake in my life. Thankfully, He was not letting go.

The Spirit of Fear

Within the first three years of my life, I had already been exposed to near death and envy. What followed closely behind was fear. Most people do not remember anything from the first few years of their lives, but I do. One of my first vivid memories is witnessing my mom and dad fighting. It is my earliest memory of the feeling of terror. We were living with my grandmother at the time, and my parents were face-to-face in a heated discussion in her kitchen. The argument ended with my mom being taken by an ambulance to the hospital. I am in my thirties now, and I still have the memory as clear as a picture. It might have been at that moment that my perception of love became one of intense passion and violence.

We can all relate to experiencing some kind of dysfunction as children; however, with spiritual opposition at work and no true knowledge of what is really behind all of the discord, many people allow havoc to reign in their homes. The Bible says we do not wrestle against flesh and blood (see Ephesians 6:12). Even though evil sometimes comes in the form of those who are flesh and blood, we have to remember there is a greater power at work. We need to tap into the power of God to know how to deal properly with evil, and we need to pray against the spirit of division. "A soft answer turns away wrath, but a harsh word stirs up anger" (Proverbs 15:1). Psalm 37:8 adds that we should "Refrain from anger, and forsake wrath! Fret not yourself: it tends only to evil."

Jesus explained what I witnessed at home. "Every kingdom divided against itself is laid waste, and no city or house divided against itself will stand" (Matthew 12:25). Despite the love my parents had for me, the anger they sometimes had toward each other made me feel as if I was not enough to bring our family together. The enemy used that against me. In God, however, His love always brings unity and peace.

Since we had no example of godly love, my family did the best we knew how. Despite everything, my parents stayed together. I have seen firsthand why the Bible tells parents not to provoke their children to anger. They are to bring them up in the discipline and instruction of the Lord, instead (see Ephesians 6:4). Had I allowed anger to lead my life, I would probably be in jail today.

The rage I witnessed, coupled with the envy I felt from those outside of my home, made me despise my life. That was exactly what the enemy wanted. He knew that if he could make me hate myself and question my identity and purpose, he could cripple me. If that happened, I would forfeit that for which God placed me on this planet. He started that attack from the beginning of my life.

Rejection of Self

Cousin Envy made sure that I had no real friends in my neighborhood. My green eyes made me stand out from my peers. The other little girls conspired against me and formed their cliques and circles without me. I spent most of my time playing outside with the little boys. This, of course, made me even less popular among the girls. But what else did I have? I had no idea what purpose was, let alone that I had one. I did not come to this awareness until I reached the age of 21. As I grew in age and comprehension, I would start to feel the spirit of fear come in the form of rejection. The resistance I felt constantly from an early age awakened the fighter in me, and it ignited my drive to survive. That drive led me ultimately into the loving arms of my Savior, Jesus Christ.

From as early as age five, I remember the sting of rejection and how it made me feel as if I were alone. I am sure every child has felt ignored or silenced at one point or another, but I always took on a more elevated feeling of rejection because of my incessant need for attention.

Since I could not get the fighting at home to stop, I thought, *Maybe they don't love me enough. Maybe I am the problem. They will not listen to my pleas for them to stop. My voice is useless.*

Among relatives, I thought, *They hate me because I look and act different. My opinions do not matter because they keep telling me to shut up.*

In school, I thought, *I'm an outcast.*

Playing in the neighborhood, I thought, *No one wants to be my friend. They are all talking about me because I am different.*

All of these lies became a part of me. For years, I believed them as truth, and they shaped my early identity. "For as he thinks within himself, so he is" (Proverbs 23:7 NASB). Because I believed the lies, Cousin Envy and rejection continued to follow me into my adulthood. Can you think of things in your early life that you believed that may not have been true? Deception is a weapon used by the enemy, the father of lies, to make us question anything and everything about our existence and purpose. He knows that our belief is the lens through which we see the world.

Before we receive any spiritual knowledge of God, our experiences are meant to shape our perception of truth. "The god of this world [Satan] has blinded the minds of the unbelievers, to keep them from seeing the light of the gospel of the glory of Christ" (2 Corinthians 4:4). It was not until recently that I identified a lot of the lies that had shaped my world. I had to replace them with God's truth about me and my purpose. Have you ever done a lie inventory in your life? If so, how many lies have shaped your life? If not, may I suggest that you take some time to do so?

Happily Never After

Because of how lonely and alienated I felt in my early life, I often found comfort in talking to myself. I used my imagination to picture the life I wished I had. I was one of the only children on my mother's side of the family, and I spent the majority of my time with those relatives. I felt so alone.

I would try to talk to the adults around me, but I was often told to stay out of grown folks' conversations. Talking to myself or acting out elaborate scenes that I saw in my imagination was all I had. I imagined a life without fighting, violence or alcohol abuse. I pretended to have the happily ever after story I saw in the movies. I also imagined being rescued by my prince charming. In my mind, my prince would be everything I ever needed. He would treat me as his queen, he would never hurt me out of anger, and he would never make me feel as if I was not enough for him.

I am not sure if it was what I saw on TV or if it was something innately inside of me, but I knew that the world was not as broken as I often witnessed it being in my environment. I imagined a world where everyone valued each other despite their differences and where love was the leading force. I think back on it now and see that God's heart was always embedded deep within me. How could a young girl believe for anything good after having witnessed the opposite so many times? I know that despite my surroundings, experiences and negative beliefs something greater was calling me.

I refused to allow hatred to break me, and I would not allow it to invade my heart. I used it to give me purpose. Optimism was a weapon I had that I did not see anyone else using. Most people called me a dreamer, and that is something I still am. I somehow always knew that not everything I saw was what it appeared to be. "Faith is the assurance of things hoped for" (Hebrews 11:1). Even though I did not know it at the time, faith kept me going. "Hope does not put us to shame, because God's love has been poured into our hearts through the Holy Spirit who has been given to us" (Romans 5:5).

I am sure that you have seen similar spiritual attacks. Although we all have unique stories, the enemy is not unique in his tactics. He uses the same attacks, which include lies, fear, deception, anger, rejection, jealousy, unforgiveness, doubt and more. His ultimate goal is to keep us separated from the love of God so that we die without salvation in Christ. It is important that you see spiritually what is really at work against you.

God has a plan, and so does the enemy. In this book, I hope to teach you how to see the spiritual world for what it is, both good and evil. I want you to realize that if God is leading, you will win!

You will find at the end of each chapter a few extra sections. First is a section of reflection. I have provided questions to prompt you to look at your life to see how the topics discussed might be expressed in your life. You will also find a section where I summarize the key takeaways from each chapter. They are listed out to help you keep your spiritual eyes open. I have also listed out a few applicable Scriptures that you can meditate on. And finally, I have written a prayer and declaration for you to speak out to the Lord.

What Do I See?

1. What early experiences do you remember that have shaped your life and what you believe?
2. Have you allowed envy or jealousy to affect you in a negative way?
3. Upon what is your definition of love based? Is it based primarily on how God defines love, what your life experiences have been or a mixture of the two?
4. List the ways that you are blessed. Make this list in spite of the negative aspects or consequences of your life.
5. Have you accepted God's truth about family, yourself and His purpose for your life?
6. How can you shift any negative atmosphere that might be in your life presently?

What Can I Learn?

- The enemy opposes God's people and tries to destroy, but God's grace causes you to live.
- The enemy targets your identity by making you hate yourself or despise your life.
- Evil will assault the innocent, so you need to be on the offense.
- Blessings attract envy and strife. Be prepared to stand strong and own your identity in Christ.
- Fear can be used in multiple ways to cripple you and make you inactive.
- Never give up hope. Choose to believe that God's best will always trump evil.

Scriptures for Meditation

John 8:44 NASB

He [the devil] was a murderer from the beginning, and does not stand in the truth because there is no truth in him. Whenever he speaks a lie, he speaks from his own nature, for he is a liar and the father of lies.

Psalm 138:7

Though I walk in the midst of trouble, you preserve my life; you stretch out your hand against the wrath of my enemies, and your right hand delivers me.

Proverbs 22:6

Train up a child in the way he should go; even when he is old he will not depart from it.

Prayer and Declaration

Father God, in the name of Jesus, I thank you for how You have protected me from the time I was in my mother's womb until now. Even though I did not always have the best example of love and peace, I know that You led me here to remind me that You have a great purpose for my life. Lord, I pray that my identity will be found in You alone—not in what I was told as a child or in what I was taught by the world. Let the source of my self-worth be Your words. I pray that You uproot every spirit of fear that has tried to cripple or short-circuit my calling in life. Also, please uproot every lie that has tried to shape my understanding, from the time of my birth until now. Please replace those lies with the truths of Your Word. Thank You for every one of Your blessings. I realize I do not deserve them, but You give them to me anyway. I am grateful! I pray for those who struggle with envy and jealousy. Lord, may their eyes be turned toward You, the rewarder of their faith. Lastly, in the midst of life's difficulties, may I never stop believing in Your greatness. May I always choose to believe that better is coming. I declare that my hope is in You. In Jesus' name, Amen.

2

God Turns Pain into Power

There will always be chaos in the world. What do you do when you find yourself in the middle of it? Are you sucked into the dysfunction of it all, or do you find a way out? In the midst of your craziest battles, God is there making a way of escape. Sometimes, the way out looks like little crumbs that you need to follow toward safety.

Your strength comes from the other side of the mayhem. In this chapter, I will share with you the pain that helped mold me into the woman of God I am today. I will share how you, too, can overcome the early traumas in your life by allowing your experiences to empower you rather than defeat you.

Superheroes Do Not Exist

This might be the hardest portion of my life to write about, because it was on this bleeding little heart that everything to follow was birthed. As a child, I pictured my home like a comic book; therefore, in the following paragraphs I will describe my home life in the style of a graphic novel.

Imagine that I am the offspring of two superheroes—Superior Man and Warrior Woman. To me, they were the strongest heroes of them all. Superior Man captivated my heart and had the ability to make me feel as if I were the only person in the world. His words, actions and deeds took precedence over everything else, and I often longed for the next moment we could be together so that I could get swept off my feet and taken on a journey through his world of oldies music and unequalled intellect and wisdom. By day, he was out saving the world. By night, he would come to headquarters, refuel and unplug from the weight of life in front of the picture box. He did this consistently Monday through Thursday.

Friday, however, was the day of dread. It seemed as if the rest of the world loved this day, but because I lived in a multiverse, I never knew in which universe I would wake up. On a good Friday, Superior Man would come home after saving the day, throw on some music and fervently sing and dance the night away. Nothing on this planet fed my little soul more. I believe that is where I began to develop my own musical superpowers. On those days, I would also ask as many questions as possible. Because of his extensive knowledge, he always had the answers.

But if I happened to wake up on a Friday in the alternate universe, Superior Man would come back to headquarters and bring his battles and his potion of weakness with him. It was a substance that had the ability to alter his state of being. Unfortunately, this substance often led to the defeat of my heroes.

Warrior Woman was my day-to-day mentor. She would send me off to learn, she would make sure I was nourished, and she would take care of all my basic training. It was her mission to look after me, so she dedicated her powers toward making sure my adventurous ways did not cause me to be harmed or captured. I always tried my hardest to impress her, but she seemed too busy making sure the headquarters were in good shape to notice me. That does not mean I quit trying to win her recognition, though.

"Warrior Woman, look at this!" I often shouted for attention. Her tasks in life must have been really hard, because she rarely took her eyes off of her responsibilities to see me for who I really was. Because of this, I focused my energy on trying to help her.

She would sometimes take off her mask and let me see her battle wounds. Warrior Woman really lived up to her name. I could never comprehend how anyone could have faced that many battles and still remained standing. In spite of that, she remained a servant and fought to continue to love even through all of the attacks that came her way.

She told me some of the heartbreaking stories behind her scars. Even though my little mind and heart could not comprehend them all, her stories began to help me develop a few superpowers of my own: wisdom, responsibility and the ability to console. I learned to use words of wisdom at the right time, and I saw that those words could bring her comfort. When I was lucky, I got to witness my words heal some of her smaller wounds. It was through helping her that I learned the principle behind the Scripture that says, "It is more blessed to give than to receive" (Acts 20:35).

Still, there was nothing I could say or do to get away from Fridays. The potion of weakness Superior Man drank had the ability to transform my biggest hero into my worst nightmare. The potion would summon Superior Man's evil alter egos, Rage and Pride, who were merciless toward him and anyone he came in contact with. With each drink, they clung tighter to him until he was consumed by them. When he was in this state, all anyone could see or hear were the alter egos. They did not care about me or Warrior Woman. Every word I said made me a target and fed the enemy that bewitched Superior Man. He could not snap out of it when the potion was around—no matter what I did.

Warrior Woman would often intervene on my behalf against Superior Man's alter egos. That is when the battles really began. She sometimes drank some of the potion of weakness, too, and instead of the potion making things better, it summoned her own evil alter egos, Hostility and Insecurity. It was during those days that I witnessed both of my heroes transform into villains. No matter how much I cried or tried to stop them from hurting each other and destroying the world around us, they did not listen. Nothing ever worked.

I began to sense when the day of dread was coming. I would wake up on those particular Fridays ready to intercept the forces of evil that caused my heroes to turn bad. It did not matter to me that I was not fully ready for battle, or that my capacity was smaller than the capacities of those I would come up against. I wanted simply to save my superheroes and get them back.

On those days, I would get home from my time of studies and wait by the front gate of headquarters. I was watching with hope that no enemies had followed Superior Man into our safe place that day. While I waited, I encountered an enemy of my own: fear. It would cause me to curl up into a little ball of anxiety and terror. That force was terribly strong. It had the power and ability to defeat me even before the battle began.

Thoughts that I had never entertained would appear suddenly in my mind. Fear put them there, and it threatened to undermine my determination. Would it also have the power to strip me of my hero powers and make me the anti-hero? Should I succumb to the evil and endure my fate and the effect it had on this world, or should I fight to get back to the universe of love and harmony? Since I was the product of two superheroes, I did not really have a choice in the matter. Fighting is what I knew, so I fought fear every time.

This is how it often went down. If I encountered the Superior Man's anti-hero on those Fridays, I would first try to use my charm and wit to steal his potion of weakness and destroy it to break its curse over him. If that was not possible, I would use my power of love and the weapon of music to try to bring him back to me. Although music had the power to unite us for a time, lamentably, that never stopped the inevitable doom.

I was not strong enough on my own to subdue the evil that infiltrated headquarters. Would I allow the anti-hero infestation to overtake me also, or would I find a way to get help? I questioned my purpose in the situation. Why would I be there to witness all of this if my abilities could not help? While I never sustained any physical wounds from these battles, each one weakened my mental and emotional strength. I became too weak eventually to carry the heartbreak.

Everyone Is in a Battle

Welcome back to reality for a moment. Take a minute to reflect on your upbringing. What was the role your parents or guardians played in your life's tale? I believe that most people experience things early in life that rob them of their innocence or their instinctual belief in the goodness of those in the world. Our experiences often cause us to withdraw, to harbor unforgiveness, or even worse, to believe in nothing good at all. These moments become attacks on our personal development and identity. But what if we recognized early that there are powers at work around us to which even our loved ones fall victim? Sometimes they need help getting free from bad situations. If we were aware of this, then I believe that we would be more equipped to face the difficult situations.

In my young mind, I had no idea these things were spiritual attacks. Pride, contention, insecurity and fear were born out of those demonic attacks. The Bible says pride comes before destruction (see Proverbs 16:18) and that we should turn away from strife (see Proverbs 20:3). Had my family known these key biblical principles, perhaps we would have been better equipped to battle the attacks that we faced.

It is important that we realize that every experience we go through has either a negative or positive impact on our lives. If we do not learn to guard our hearts, then we are susceptible to the lies of the enemy. "Above all else, guard your heart, for everything you do flows from it" (Proverbs 4:23 NIV).

What I did not know at the time was that regardless of how strong and mighty Superior Man was, he was sad deep inside. His sadness went far back to a time before Warrior Woman and I were in his life. In the early stages of his training, he had not experienced a safe haven. Among all those in his tribe of heroes, he stood apart. He was different and held great power within. That power was something that was despised among his peers.

After years of not being accepted by his own people, he was left to find his own way. He first tried the potion of weakness, thinking it would make him stronger; however, before he realized what it was really doing to him, he became enchanted by its spell. Along the way, he met Warrior Woman. While they were different from each other, she believed in his abilities as no one else had.

Eventually, they began to make a tribe of their own. Even though he tried to focus on training up his own little heroes, the potion of weakness made it difficult for him to build safe headquarters. Because the potion was the only thing that Superior Man knew would numb his sadness, he used it without realizing that it was actually what his enemy was using to weaken him and destroy his tribe.

Warrior Woman had a completely different upbringing. Her training happened within a very sheltered space that housed no patriarch. When she met Superior Man, she gave him that role freely and followed his lead.

As they trained me and I began to experience my own battles, I remembered something Superior Man taught me early on. He told me that there is a source from which all of our combined powers come: Creator. It took some time for me to understand Creator's role in everything, but I discovered eventually that He is where I needed to turn during my days of dread. I first started looking to Creator after I saw Superior Man and Warrior Woman dangling outside of a window just moments away from death. It was a scenario in which their forces collided. It could have ended pretty badly, but—thank God—the battle ended before the worst happened. I really needed backup that day, and who better to intervene than Creator?

Because of my age and ignorance, I had no way of directly accessing Creator. I started to send out what I thought of as rescue signals. I often used tears as my point of access. Once I established communication, I sent out my signal. Eventually, this would happen every night. I lived in anticipation that the day of dread was coming. I figured that if my tears created a flood then maybe, just maybe, Creator would send me a raft, and I would be able to escape this multiverse with both of my heroes in tow.

I never saw Creator during those times, but I know now that He was there. I know that He always had the final say. Time and time again, Superior Man and Warrior Woman would come back to their senses and to each other, and I know He helped them do that. Helping them come back became my first life's mission. It stayed my mission until the day that I left headquarters to find my own place of refuge.

I shared my story in this manner because of how hard it is to verbalize what I witnessed and felt as a child. But I know that what my little heart and mind endured helped me to see life from an eternal perspective. I knew intuitively that there had to be more to life than the cycle of dysfunction that I had experienced.

Experience Is Your Superpower

In this day and age people tend to believe that life just happens. They believe that people are flawed, that they suck, that they disappoint and that simply is the way it is. I, however, challenge that way of thinking. The Bible says there is good in everything He created (see Genesis 1:31). Was His creation no longer good after the devil deceived Adam and Eve and they gave in to temptation? Sure, sin has consequences, but Adam and Eve were made in the image of God. Their lives continued on, and God still pursued a connection with them. Despite their failure and the fact that they allowed the enemy to deceive them, God still used them to populate the world. We see over and over again in Scripture that people mess up, but God still uses those broken people to do extraordinary things in His name.

The key thing to remember in failure is that you have to get back up. You cannot stay in the place of defeat and be used by God. You cannot harbor unforgiveness toward those who should have protected you and expect to walk in freedom. As we see in the examples of the superheroes in my life, that pattern does not produce anything but more pain and added hurt.

Have you been disappointed beyond belief in your past, in your family situation and in what happened to you? Me, too. I get it. But the enemy uses all of these problems to introduce you to another enemy—self-pity. Instead of dusting ourselves off and getting up, we invite self-pity to slow dance with us, thinking we will feel better. It will not happen.

Having a pity party is like throwing a party to which no one is invited—not even Jesus—because you are too busy feeling bad for yourself. I am not trying to minimize pain or disappointment, but we must learn to grieve it, release it and then use it to strengthen ourselves and those with whom we interact.

Superheroes do not exist in the way we see on TV. Those we love or idolize will fail us at some point. If you are not vigilant, the enemy will use those failures to lay down the groundwork of his plot in your life. He will take everything from you eventually, if you let him. We have to remain dependent on God and ask Him for grace when dealing with others. We are not to have confidence in man.

We have to learn that we do not get over the moments easily that scar us as children. But it is when we analyze these memories that we see that God—and God alone—is the true superhero who saves the day. Only God can reach down deep enough to give us the grace we need to get through the trauma we face in life. I am encouraged when I read, "When you pass through the waters, I will be with you; and through the rivers, they shall not overwhelm you; when you walk through fire you shall not be burned, and the flame shall not consume you" (Isaiah 43:2).

Many people hide away their bad experiences. Eventually, however, something will trigger their trauma, and they will find themselves crippled by distress. Suppressed memories are like haunting melodies that are on repeat. Unless you go through them with God and get the closure that only He can give, you will spend your life listening to their familiar tunes. You have to go back into your memories, with God by your side, and receive healing for those hard moments to which the enemy tries to keep you chained.

The forces of darkness know that if they can infect the family structure with their evil ways, then generations will be affected. In therapy, counselors have a tool called a genogram. It is a family map that leads clients through their family's history of interaction. This tool helps people discover patterns within their generational lines. People do not often think about the divorce rate in their family, for instance.

But if they were to map out and document their family's divorce history, they would often be shocked to see how history continues to repeat itself. That is, until someone decides to change the pattern.

You will find that the more vulnerable you are with God and the greater access you give Him, the more freedom you have. Reliving the stories of my own life has not been easy for me. In completing the process of writing this out, I have seen some areas of trauma that I have yet to walk through with Jesus. As hard as that is, I am glad to be uncovering them so that I can invite God to help me through.

If you have noticed that you still have some areas of brokenness that need to be addressed, please take them to God for healing. Ask Him to help you see Him as the hero of your story, even if that story has some really bad characters in it. Remove the expectations you have put on those who should have known better. I often think of the moment that Jesus was on the cross. He looked out at the very people He came to save as they were celebrating His torture and death.

He could have said, "Father, they know better. Father, how could they?" Instead He said, "Father, forgive them, for they know not what they do" (Luke 23:34). Jesus laid down His life willingly that day. Even while He was on the cross, He was an example to us of how to deal with those who fail us. The characters in our stories have experienced their own traumas, and sometimes they are not strong enough to allow God into their pain to heal them. We have to break the pattern of that right now, and we have to allow ourselves to learn from our pain.

What Do I See?

1. What used to be the fairytale view you had of your life?
2. How did you react once you realized that reality is different from what we see on TV?
3. How have you allowed yourself to heal?
4. How have you released and forgiven those who have hurt you?

What Can I Learn?

- Sometimes the people closest to us and who should love us the most end up hurting us the most. We have to forgive them.
- The way that authority figures treat us is not a reflection of how God feels about us.
- We must draw our strength to fight life's battles from God. Turning to a substance or another flawed human will disappoint.
- Do not allow the attacks of the enemy to invade your safe space. Be alert, on guard and fight back with the Word of God.
- Invite Christ into your crisis, whether you sense He is there or not. He always saves the day.

Scriptures for Meditation

Psalm 27:10 NLT
Even if my father and mother abandon me, the Lord will
hold me close.

Ephesians 6:4
Fathers, do not provoke your children to anger, but bring
them up in the discipline and instruction of the Lord.

Psalm 34:18
The Lord is near to the brokenhearted and saves the crushed
in spirit.

Isaiah 43:2
When you pass through the waters, I will be with you; and
through the rivers, they shall not overwhelm you; when you
walk through fire you shall not be burned, and the flame
shall not consume you.

Prayer and Declaration

Father, I thank You that even when the world around
me fails, I have You to rescue and save me. Lord, may
You reach down deep and heal my broken heart. As
I go back into my past to identify the areas that have
scarred me, it is not always easy. I bring to You my disappointments, my traumas and my expectations. Help
me to forgive as Jesus did, and help me to see You as
my superhero and my everything. I release those around

me from the expectations that I had of them, and I look to You, the author and finisher of my faith. My strength comes from You, and in You I can overcome any of life's hardest battles. Reveal to me the experiences I have suppressed, and help me to walk through those painful moments with You. God, be my source of power. May my identity be rewritten by You and what You say about me. In Jesus' name, Amen.

3

What You Cannot See Can Hurt You

The enemy tries to create strongholds in our lives by using those who are closest to us. If you are unaware of this scheme, you can allow generational curses to afflict you. This can happen even when those curses have nothing to do with you or are not a result of what you have done. You must renounce the curses and ask God to break them off of you and the generations that follow you. Breaking off generational curses can be as simple as making a declaration that your allegiance is no longer to your family line or to those who came before you. Declare that you and the generations who follow are now linked to God and His plan for your life, for your children's lives and for your children's children's lives. For some, the ties to one's family lineage can be so strong that they might need to employ extra steps of faith to sever the ties. Enlisting prayer from others, fasting or warring spiritually against any demonic stronghold might be required to keep you from repeating the evil patterns of your ancestors.

In this chapter, I will share with you the importance of establishing your own foundational belief systems outside of tradition, and why it is important that you renounce demonic ties. What you believe forms your life, so it is important to take personal inventory and establish what it is you are truly rooted in.

Evil Creeps In

Despite being known as the Puerto Rican girl with nice eyes, whose parents threw her the best birthday parties on the block, I found myself craving attention desperately. Maybe it was because the recognition I desired was nonexistent, or that I did not grow up with my older siblings or that I was the only child in my extended family, but I felt lonely. I had no real friends in the neighborhood or at school. It was during this time that I became sensitive to the spiritual realm. I felt lonelier than ever, and the spirit of isolation crept in.

I realized that this process of heightened spiritual awareness was growing when I saw a vision of an African man standing on my fire escape. The man I saw I had seen previously in an image at one of my family's Santería religious feasts. Santería, my maternal family religion, is of Yoruba lineage and originates in Cuba among West African descendants. For some who practice the religion, Santería also has Roman Catholic influences that including the veneration of saints.

The ancient religious customs of the Yoruba people are what those who practice the religion today still observe.

This includes going into a trance, which is a divination system meant to communicate with the dead, the ancestors, or "Orishas," the human form of spirits. People who practice Santería also perform animal sacrifices, cut themselves, conduct rituals, dress in all white, smoke cigars and throw lavish parties with spirit-inspired drumming, dancing, food and drinks that are then offered to the dead spirits who are conjured by the followers.

Babalú-Ayé, who I understood to be the head honcho of the Orishas, is considered "Father, Lord of the Earth." He is associated heavily with healing and punishing through disease. I cannot tell you how many times I heard people in this religion curse the health of others. Babalú was the man I would occasionally see standing on my fire escape staring at me through my window—or at least I believed it was him. At first, I kept the appearance of the man to myself, but the spirit continued to manifest. I recall being paralyzed by fear as he stared into my little soul. If I turned away or tried to get my mom's attention, he would vanish.

I also began having horrific night terrors, waking up in the middle of the night screaming and scaring my parents half to death. I once awoke from a bad dream to see the illusion of hundreds of bugs crawling all over me. As I screamed for my father to get them all off, he looked at me with eyes of worry and explained that there was nothing on me. I was wide-awake seeing insects, but they were not physically there. I wonder if I was seeing in the spiritual realm and that is why it felt real to me. The spiritual realm is far more real than what our natural eyes behold.

On occasion, my dad would read to me from a children's Bible his mother had given me. That is when I started to realize there was something a lot greater at work in this world. I recall the stories of creation, Adam and Eve, the deception of the serpent and the crazy miracles of Moses demonstrating God's power to the pharaoh of Egypt. We never quite made it to Jesus in the New Testament, but I first learned of good and evil as dad read to me from that Bible.

One time after reading with my dad, I remember lying next to him as he turned to watch TV in our railroad-style apartment in Brooklyn, New York. All of a sudden, the walls stretched about a mile long. My mom was in the kitchen, which now appeared to be a long distance away from me, and I began shouting for her. When my father turned to see what was wrong with me, I did not understand why he could not see what I was seeing. After about thirty seconds everything was back to normal. I, however, was left terrified and confused, feeling like a freak and more isolated than ever.

I believe that living in New York City comes with a unique spiritual fight. The oppressive principality over the area is felt all around. From anxiety caused by all of the hustle and bustle, including the struggle to survive and the cutthroat dog-eat-dog attitude that makes everyone angry, to the gray, gloomy filter that is seen over the city. Even in all of that there was a glimpse of light for me.

I met a crazy white man, named Bill Wilson, who spearheaded a youth ministry that has since gone worldwide. I say crazy because he went unapologetically into the heart of the ghetto with a yellow school bus and a bullhorn every Saturday. His mission was to pick up inner-city kids and take them to his ministry, Metro World Child. To us kids, it was better known as Yogi Bear Sunday school. I had no idea what Sunday school was, and it certainly did not feel like church to me. My experiences with church had been stained-glass windows, repetitive prayers, standing up, kneeling and sitting down. I enjoyed Yogi Bear Sunday school greatly, and I respected Pastor Bill deeply. Whenever he would drive down my street with a bullhorn blaring, all of the neighborhood kids would run out to catch the bus.

While at Yogi Bear, we would hear inspiring stories, sing hilarious songs and win prizes. It was like Christmas morning every week for those of us who desperately needed hope. The only time we would get serious during the service was when Pastor Bill, who was an orphan and had been abandoned as a kid on the side of the road, would teach us how to pray to God. I did not know it at the time, but it was that teaching that would help me through the dark season of my youth.

I now had a tool in my arsenal against the wicked schemes of the enemy. I had learned how to pray, which allowed me to communicate with God about anything. For many years I cried out to God praying for my broken home or for a real friend, all the while still being tormented by my dreams and seeing people or things that were not really there. I knew I had to rely on the discipline of prayer, so I did.

Through prayer, you have the ability to ask God to assign spiritual beings to fight off the evil spirits who are trying to lead you astray. Prayer invites the supernatural into the natural, and I believe it is the most powerful Christian practice there is. Psalm 57 reveals the effect that prayer can have not only on earth but also in the spiritual realm. "I cry out to God Most High, to God who fulfills his purpose for me. He will send from heaven and save me; he will put to shame him who tramples on me. God will send out his steadfast love and his faithfulness!" (verses 2–3).

Dedication to Santería

At the same time that all of this was happening, my mom decided to take me to see the family sorcerer, who was considered a high priestess in Santería. She walked confidently in her authority of being the "family witch," as she would say. She explained to my mom that all of the visions I was having meant that my spiritual awakening had come and that spiritism was choosing me.

I was a very young girl when the high priestess came to our apartment one weeknight and instructed me to go in the bathroom and strip off all of my clothes. When I was finished, I walked out to a dark home that was illuminated only by candles. A mini tub awaited me in the center of my mother's kitchen, and I was told to step inside. I walked uncomfortably to the tub, trying to cover my private parts, and stepped in. I was among family, so I felt that I had no choice but to trust them.

The high priestess proceeded to pour on me Agua de Florida (a cologne used by shamans for cleansing, healing, ritual feeding and flowering). She also poured onto me some other substances, blew cigar smoke over me from head to toe, and used a machete to crack open a coconut and some other fruits over my head as she performed her ritual.

This ceremony would serve as a "purification" ritual into the religion. Once completed, I was given a multicolored beaded necklace known as a *collare* (KOH-jah-r). I was told to wear it every day for protection. The collare represents five of seven African powers. Each spiritual intermediary holds a different position in the supernatural realm, and, according to the high priestess, the one that governs "love" and the "sweet waters," named Ochún, was assigned to me.

But these powers are actually spiritual strongholds that bind people to a spirit other than God.

The ritual would now make the high priestess my godmother, and from that moment on it would be her duty to look after me and my life. She instructed us to put a cup of water by the entrance of our house as a way to keep evil away and to have me sleep with a camphor block in my pillow for spiritual protection. Unfortunately, my nightmares only got worse.

Notice that this purification ceremony modeled itself as a mock Christian baptism. By the end of the ceremony, a spirit of that religion is given governance over the new convert. Whoever leads the ceremony is then supposed to serve as a mentor to the one being indoctrinated, similar to what a pastor would do with someone he is discipling. At the time, I had no idea what true Christianity was, so I reluctantly embraced my family's religion. I also started Catholic classes for Communion, known as the Confraternity of Christian Doctrine, or CCD. This was also a tradition in my family.

The spiritual realm was being opened to me at an early age in a greater way than most. This ethereal, spiritual reality that was unseen by most human eyes was becoming my reality. At this time in my life, the war for my little soul had kicked into high gear. Looking back, I see how God had His holy angels always guiding me. Whether it was Yogi Bear Sunday school, my grandma's Bible gift, CCD classes or my new practice of praying, there was always a glimmer of light in my life.

After my dedication to Santería, the religious necklace I was given kept breaking, and I could not figure out why. During a sleepover with a neighbor, I removed my collare as we were preparing to go to bed. As I went to hang it on my headpost, it shattered in my hands and scattered all over the floor. My friend and I were baffled, and we had no idea how it had been possible for a necklace to burst right before our eyes. My mom and I never said anything about it after that day, but we had an unspoken understanding that I was not meant to wear that necklace. From that point on, I never did.

Traps of the Enemy

My dedication to that religion, nonetheless, did not end. My high priestess godmother grew more intentional about inviting me and my mom to her parties for the dead. These parties included an altar that was filled with voodoo-looking dolls that honored the African spirit who was their leader. They served food and drink to an altar dedicated to him, and those practicing the faith would dress all in white, except on the sacred holiday of Halloween.

Before the celebration would commence, they would smoke cigars, and the high priestess would sacrifice a white dove and hang it somewhere. Many times, the chief spiritist would conjure a spirit and then speak in a type of tongues. Her eyes would roll back and she would single out different people. I remember her talking in an incomprehensible language to individual people, but never would there be an interpretation of the spiritual language spoken.

I had no idea that this ceremony twisted Judeo-Christian past or present practices. The nation of Israel, for example, also practiced sacrificing animals and bringing food and drink to God (see Leviticus 4:35; Numbers 15:4). People first spoke in different tongues on the Day of Pentecost, and Christians continue to use this gift of the Holy Spirit today (see Acts 2; 19:1–20; 1 Corinthians 12–14). What I did know is that I wanted no part of Santería's practices, and I definitely did not feel safe. In fact, I was scared.

Some of the things I witnessed were truly disturbing. I remember watching them writing people's names on a paper bag, sewing it on a store-bought pig's tongue and then dumping it into the ocean as some kind of a curse on those whose names were written on the bag. Thank God that when we come to Him, He renews our minds and does not give us a spirit of fear. Instead, He gives us a spirit of power and love and self-control (see 2 Timothy 1:7). If it was not for God's renewing power, I would probably still have night terrors.

The Bible is very clear about all of these evil practices, but people think they know better than God. "Do not turn to mediums or necromancers; do not seek them out, and so make yourselves unclean by them: I am the LORD your God" (Leviticus 19:31). Galatians 5:20 lists sorcery or witchcraft as one of the works of the flesh that will prevent people from inheriting the Kingdom of God. Being exposed to witchcraft in my adolescence helped me understand the importance of guarding myself against contact with the unknown spiritual realm.

I once witnessed a relative's house that was completely bewitched by a spirit who slammed her cupboards and drawers in the middle of the night. During one of my sleepovers at her house, one of her statues summoned me with a sound. It was late at night and I woke up to use the bathroom. I started hearing the sound of castanets that drew me to a religious altar that was in display at the house. Creepily enough it was coming from a hollow statue of Oshun, the stronghold that was assigned to me by my high priestess godmother. I had goosebumps everywhere. When I picked up the statue, the sound that had been coming from the inside of it stopped. I was most freaked out because the inside of the statue was completely hollow. It was empty.

I would never advise you to make contact with a demonic idol. In fact, I advise you to rebuke and reject anything that is not of God. Declare God's protection over your life. Tell that demon it has no power over you in Jesus' name!

Around this time, my spiritist godmother also insisted on giving me a card reading. I have heard many people say that seeing psychics is harmless and a form of entertainment. But from my experience with my godmother, who also moonlit as a gypsy who read cards, I know that opening yourself up to someone who engages actively with the spirit realm is opening yourself to an entire spiritual world of demons who then have a point of access into your life. The things she prophesied while reading the cards were terrifying. According to her tarot reading, I would be raped, hit by a car and end up alone at the end of my life. Who would want to live after that? I am sure all of those things were seeds sown by the enemy to break my spirit and invite the spirit of suicide into my life.

Give Evil No Power

As she prophesied those evil words to me, I remembered something my father told me when I asked him if he believed in my mom's family religion. He said, "I don't give any of it power over me, so it cannot touch me." I do not know why he took that position toward Santería, but I made that same declaration after the card reading. By the grace of God, none of those things have taken place in my life, and they never will, in Jesus' name. We do not have to accept everything that comes to us. The Bible says that we should "not believe every spirit, but test the spirits to see whether they are from God, for many false prophets have gone out into the world" (1 John 4:1).

I believe many people who have a supernatural gift of prophecy or a heightened sense of the supernatural were meant to be prophets for God. Then the enemy enchanted them to use their gifts for him instead. Look how hard the enemy was gunning for me to be intrigued by his antics. Acts 16:16–19 tells the story of a young girl who had a spirit of divination and who was making a lot of money by fortune telling. The apostle Paul cast the spirit out of her, which in turn set her free.

I find that most people who serve as mediums or seers are enslaved to the monetary benefit of fortune telling without factoring in their eternal security. My spiritist godmother was always so desperate to make money by reading people's futures that she did not entertain any other options by which she could support herself. Despite some of the scary things that my godmother did, I gravitated toward her because she had shown me more love than anyone else. If it was not for my God-given discernment, I would not have suspected that anything that happened during this season of my life was wrong. I trusted my family to lead me safely.

Obviously, your friends and family are not Satan. But the devil knows how to reach us through those we trust or through those who give off an appearance of good but who lack character. The Bible warns us, "Even Satan disguises himself as an angel of light" (2 Corinthians 11:14). I believe in the authority of rejecting the lies of the enemy, which was both what my dad told me as a child and what I have experienced as an adult. "Death and life are in the power of the tongue" (Proverbs 18:21). Had I accepted those things spoken over me by my godmother, who knows if they would have happened.

Seeds of Light

While all of this was going on, I was also attending CCD classes at my childhood Catholic church. I was intrigued by this God who died for me. Seeds of truth were being sown as I learned a bit more about Jesus. I was also intrigued by the church's priest, Father Brescia, who had been recently transferred to us from another country. He had the godliest character I had encountered. He emanated the love of God to all of the people in my neighborhood who desperately needed hope.

When Father Brescia realized that I had an interest in learning about God, he took me under his wing. Before I knew it, I was learning church songs and was the only kid invited to sing with the worship team on Sundays. Sadly, Father Brescia was only passing through, and he was assigned to another church after about a year. His brief impact on my life was surely another seed of light in my very dark world. While the enemy was at work, God was counteracting the plans the enemy had for me. God sent seeds of light to guide me toward Himself.

As you reflect on the spiritual activity in my early life, does it bring up memories of what the enemy may have done in your past to lure you into bondage? The only spirit that should come upon you is the Holy Spirit. The Holy Spirit is called holy to help us distinguish between God's Spirit and evil spirits, some of whom are seeking to create strongholds in your life.

A stronghold is something that holds on and does not want to let go. I have always envisioned it as a bouncer at the door of a nightclub who will not let the people get out. In order for you to get out of that place you will have to pummel the strong man and find your way to freedom. God fights the strong man for you, causing you to find your way to victory with the least amount of damage. God warned the people of Israel not to be enticed by the pagan practices of the surrounding nations, and in doing so fall into their sins (see Leviticus 18:26–30; Deuteronomy 12:29–31; 18:9). But this is what led eventually to their captivity (see 2 Kings 17:8–16). God calls Himself a jealous God (see Exodus 20:5) who is eager that His people remain loyal to Him. Many of the customs passed down through generations are not of God. Those evil practices, however, do not have to be our story. I often pray for God to start my family lineage with me, because I am a first-generation Christian. I pray for all those who come after me to be blessed and used by God— and not the evil one. We do not have to subscribe to ungodly advice or practices that are taught to us, nor do we have to inherit the curses of our ancestors.

The Holy Spirit always emanates Christ and gives us the ability to walk in God's ways. An angel or spirit being from God should be a reflection of God, and it should give full glory to the Most High. If you think that you might be entertaining an angel or spiritual being, you should test it against that standard. Anything that does not meet those qualifications comes from the demonic realm and should be shunned.

What Do I See?

1. What family practices might have influenced you spiritually but are not purely of God?
2. What kind of interaction have you had with enchanters, psychics, spiritualists, mediums, or even something as "simple" as a horoscope?
3. What effects do you see from these influences? Have you renounced those practices and generational ties?

What Can I Learn?

- Witchcraft is real and mocks Christianity. The enemy tries to establish a stronghold in our lives by using those closest to us. Do not partake in witchcraft or spiritual exercises, because it leaves an open door to an unforgiving spiritual realm.
- Generational curses can afflict you even when they have nothing to do with you or what you have done.
- When dealing with spiritual experiences, go to Jesus for clarity or deliverance. Do not rely on the traditions of men. (I wonder what would have happened if my mom had taken me to church instead of taking me to the family witch.)
- Witchcraft and evil can mimic godly truths and Christian practices, but they are always distorted and a perversion of the truth.
- God will always counteract evil. Look for light in the darkest moments.

- Do not accept the lies from the enemy. Speak life over yourself.
- Renounce, repent and break spiritual ties and generational curses to be free.

Scriptures for Meditation

Isaiah 8:19 NLT

Someone may say to you, "Let's ask the mediums and those who consult the spirits of the dead. With their whisperings and mutterings, they will tell us what to do." But shouldn't people ask God for guidance? Should the living seek guidance from the dead?

Ephesians 6:12–13 NKJV

For we do not wrestle against flesh and blood, but against principalities, against powers, against the rulers of the darkness of this age, against spiritual hosts of wickedness in the heavenly places. Therefore take up the whole armor of God, that you may be able to withstand in the evil day, and having done all, to stand.

James 4:7

Submit yourselves therefore to God. Resist the devil, and he will flee from you.

Prayer and Declaration

Father God, in the name of Jesus, I give my life to You —my past, present and future. I turn away from all evil influences, and I ask You to uproot and break every generational curse over me and my family. I renounce every tie to Satan and spirits that are not Your Holy Spirit, and I pray that You would be Lord and master of my existence. Baptize me with Your Holy Spirit and let Your light dispel the darkness in my life, my home, my neighborhood and everywhere I go. I close every door to the enemy and his demons, and I walk fearlessly in Your authority and Your covering. You are the one true God and are solely in control of my fate. Every word spoken against me I condemn, and no weapon formed against me shall prosper, because You are my strong tower. I take shelter under Your shadow, and I am under Your protection and guidance. In Jesus' name, Amen.

4

Who Are You Listening To?

Many people do not realize the impact that media can have on a person's soul. Our eyes and ears serve as portals that allow things into our spirits. What you feed your spirit is important. Take music, for instance. Music can single-handedly be used to help lift the spirit, heal a heart or even release chemicals that make the body react a certain way. We all have a choice in what we allow to have an impact on us. Are the things that you are allowing into your sphere leading you to freedom in life, or are they adding to the enemy's plan to destroy you? In this chapter, we will explore the ways both God and the devil used my love for music to have an impact on my life, and I will provide some tips on how you can protect yourself from listening to the wrong tune.

Whispers from the Enemy

As time went on, not much changed. Fear and envy increased in my life, and the prophecy that my spiritist relative spoke over my life hovered over my head. I used all of the negative things that were happening in my world as an opportunity to condemn myself. Every one of those thoughts was an assignment from the enemy of my soul that he used to continue to write the "I hate Jeannie" narrative. Unfortunately, I fell for it every time.

I cannot remember exactly when it began, but I was only in my single digits when the enemy first introduced me to his ultimate plan for me. He revealed to me the king of all his tactics—death. He started to whisper to me that things would be better if I ended my life. Because I had heard about suicide on TV and in adult conversations, the devil was able to capitalize on that knowledge.

One day, after a big blowup in my home in which I failed again to bring peace, I sat in my tub for a bath. I tried to distract myself by playing with my dolls. While there, thoughts kept coming to my mind. *Maybe everyone would stop fighting if I killed myself. I could slit my wrist right now, and the tragedy would bring unity.* My heart was broken, and the enemy used my sadness as an opportunity to put these suggestions in my head. He gave me irrational thoughts that, at the time, seemed as if they made sense. I remember looking over at my mother's razors and contemplating how I would do it. This scenario played out several times during this phase of my life.

As these thoughts kept plaguing me, I got to the point where I held the razor in my hand. It was as if there was a loud voice saying, *Just do it. Show them how much you are hurting.* Deep inside, however, I knew that there was something else contending for my life. I had to strain hard to hear it, but it assured me that there was more to life than what I was experiencing currently. Thankfully, I never went through with suicide. The softer inner voice is almost always that voice of reason, but it is often ignored because life gets very loud. God spoke to Elijah in "a still small voice" (1 Kings 19:12 KJV), and He sometimes does that with us. It is important that we listen for that voice.

The Root of Suicidal Thoughts

Some thoughts of suicide and depression come from a chemical imbalance in the brain, and some have roots that begin in the heart. Unforgiveness, doubt, unresolved feelings and anger are some conditions that can aid the path for rebel spirits to insert suicidal thoughts into unsuspecting minds. Those feelings are notes in a composition that is meant to make you feel worse about yourself and your life. The more you listen to those thoughts and feelings, the easier it will be for them to lead you down a merciless path that ends in destruction. We have to remember that the devil is crafty, but he is not all-powerful.

In Psalm 13:2–4, King David prays for God to help him out of the sorrow he is feeling, because he knew that his broken heart would give the devil place to overcome him:

> How long must I take counsel in my soul and have sorrow in my heart all the day? How long shall my enemy be exalted over me? Consider and answer me, O LORD my God; light up my eyes, lest I sleep the sleep of death, lest my enemy say, "I have prevailed over him," lest my foes rejoice because I am shaken.

Like David, who was referred to as a man after God's own heart (see Acts 13:22), Jesus provides us an example of what to do when we are in despair. In the Garden of Gethsemane, He told His disciples, "My soul is very sorrowful, even to death" (Matthew 26:38; Mark 14:34). Following this, He went away to pray. He was in such anguish that He sweat drops of blood. Still, He looked to the Father who He knew could give Him the strength to fulfill the purpose He had on earth. What should you do when you are feeling down and are beyond consolation? Do what Jesus did, and pray for God's strength to pick you up and help you complete all that He has called you to do.

As a child I did not know that I could pray against my negative thoughts of suicide, so God helped me find refuge another way. I did not share these stories with anyone until I was older, because that is when I finally realized what had been going on in my little soul. God was always there battling that loud devil and giving me another option. Some might say that it was reason, logic or my gut instinct, but I know that it was God because of how hopeless and alone I had felt. If God had not given me the grace to do so, I would have had no other reason to live.

Release the Brokenness and Heal

One of the graces used to help save my life as a child was music. I had no idea that gospel or Christian music existed. God used what I had access to, which was the popular music of the time. I thank God for artists such as Mariah Carey who were not afraid to be vulnerable in their music. That resonates with me. I remember begging my mother to buy me

Mariah Carey's latest album, *Daydream*, on cassette tape. I was enamored by her voice and musical style throughout the whole album, but it was not until I reached the final track that I was really touched. The song is called "Looking In," and it addresses Carey's feelings of having felt like an outcast and having battled loneliness since her childhood.

As I listened to her voice and lyrics I began to weep. I was a little girl, and perhaps I could not comprehend everything she was saying, but the brokenness she talked about was exactly how I felt. Before that moment I had not been able to articulate the pain in my heart, I had never felt relief from my pain, and I had never known the power that music possessed to heal. I listened to that song over and over. I made myself cry it all out until the feelings of despair and suicide dissipated. Mariah inspired me beyond words. She felt how I felt but still made something of her life. That idea completely shifted the trajectory of my life. I now had a reason to live. As a result, I wanted others to know that music had the power to help them make it out, because it had helped me make it out.

The dreamer in me was awakened, and it silenced the voice that had been telling me to end my life. I had a purpose, and I was determined to get out of my current situation. As an adult looking back, I can see clearly what had been happening in the spiritual realm. I had been ambushed repeatedly, and the enemy wanted to keep me from seeing what would happen if I used my pain as power. Initially, all that I could see and feel was the grief I felt. I replayed the traumas I had experienced over and over. Those memories were like a broken record that stayed stuck in one place so that it could not play the rest of the song.

Have you had moments when you kept replaying your most difficult experiences, and because of that you remained stuck? Well, that is where I was until God threw me a lifeline. Music translates pain. Mariah did that for herself, and that had an impact on me. I was now determined to sing and write songs that could translate what I was feeling so that I could free myself and others. I needed an outlet, and from that moment until this day music has been that for me.

Had I not allowed that song to pierce my soul and minister to my brokenness, perhaps I would have stayed stuck in that broken record. I urge you to break free from replaying the hurt over and over. It is a trap that the enemy utilizes. He uses our instinct of feeling sorry for ourselves to trap us so that we do not move on to better. Instead, we should use our pain as a steppingstone to help get us out of bad situations.

Sing a New Song

"When the righteous cry for help, the LORD hears and delivers them out of all of their troubles" (Psalm 34:17). Other than my tears, I had no way of communicating with God; however, the Bible assures me that because of my broken heart and crushed spirit He was near. In my situation, God used music to get my attention.

I approached my dad and told him I believed I was born to be a famous singer, and I wanted to help others through music. He told me immediately that if this was the route I wanted to take, I would have to learn how to write songs. He placed a notepad and pen in front of me and began to teach me the art of songwriting. My dad was not a professional musician, but he was certainly an avid music listener. Some of my best memories with him are when we listened to music in our living room area, singing and dancing the night away.

My first attempt at writing was a love song. My dad asked me what I wanted to talk about, and since I was afraid to share what was really in my heart, I told him about a crush I had. We titled the song "Shy Like Me." I still remember it. Songwriting brought a temporary peace to my home, and my dad was glad that I had come to him for help with my new dream.

We wrote a few more songs together before I felt confident enough to write a song of my own about what was really in my heart. Most of my songs were about surviving and living for greater days. If you listen to my music today, I write in the style of an overcomer. I still believe music can be used for a greater good.

Destruction through Distraction

As I began to become more involved with music, I became a fan of music from the nineties. I listened to whatever was playing on mainstream radio and watched the music videos on MTV. Unfortunately, the power of music works both ways. As I became exposed to different types of modern music, I also became influenced by it. Some of the rhythms were enticing and caused me to want to explore different sides of myself. The music opened up my curiosity about many things, including sexuality, though I was never into drinking or drugs.

Heartfelt music was what reached me the most, and I was ready to show everyone around me that making music was what I was created to do. My parents gave me a karaoke machine, and I went door to door asking my neighbors in our apartment building if they would like to hear me sing a song. My voice was not at all developed, but because I could carry a tune, they humored me.

I was determined to become famous as a singer, so I enrolled in my school chorus and continued performing mini concerts for my neighborhood. It is amazing where determination can lead. In a few years I would become a professional, full-time musician. I now had something to live for, and the suicidal thoughts were silenced. The enemy, therefore, had to switch his strategy to try to get me distracted. Keep in mind that the evil one uses the same tactics with us all. He attacks our identity, he uses our insecurities against us and he uses others who cross our paths. His end goal is always to destroy us or to have us destroy ourselves.

His most cunning scheme, I believe, is to get us distracted. Although God used music to save my life and to get my focus off the trauma that I had experienced in my young life, I would soon become distracted with my new dream and the wonder of entertainment. Those things created a wall between me and God. Until I reached my twenties, the joy of entertaining distracted me to the point that I did not realize that He had a plan for my life. Ezekiel hints that before Satan, who was once called Lucifer, was cast out of heaven, he was involved with music. "The workmanship of your timbrels and pipes was prepared for you on the day you were created" (Ezekiel 28:13 NKJV). Needless to say, the evil one knows a thing or two about how to use music to his advantage.

"For I know the plans I have for you, declares the LORD, plans for welfare and not for evil, to give you a future and a hope" (Jeremiah 29:11). God spoke these words to Jeremiah, but He has a plan for all of us as well. At the time, however, I was being taught by mainstream media that it was my job to make and create my own destiny. The American dream was being ingrained in me by what I listened to and watched. God was on reserve in case I needed Him. The artists I listened to were all about glorifying themselves, sex or rebellion, and since music became my escape, it also became my number one influencer.

I like to describe entertainment as having the role of preachers and worship leaders in a lot of people's lives—especially those like young Jeannie—who allow music, movies or TV to mold their personalities and shape their goals. Has what you have listened to or watched ever had an impact on you? Have you noticed yourself emulating something after watching it on screen? Or have you heard a beat and noticed that your body started to move automatically? That is the power of influence. The problem is that if you do not feed yourself with positive things and the life-giving words of God, you will eventually realize you have been listening to the wrong preachers and worshiping the wrong things.

If you look up the word *worship* you will find that it is derived from the word *weorthscipe*. This means the act of deeming something worthy enough to give your worth to it. Although it sometimes seems as if we do not give worth to harmless entertainment, we must be mindful of what we are indoctrinating ourselves with. Entertainment is often what teaches us.

Remember, if the enemy cannot destroy you one way, he will find another way to destroy you. One of those ways is to get you distracted. Many times, we give him free rein by the doors we open through the movies we watch, the music we listen to or the TV shows we see. I cannot, for example, expect to have sweet dreams or be as bold as a lion if I watch horror films that were created to scare me and disturb my peace. Likewise, if I want to refrain from using filthy language, I should not listen to music that is filled with curses. I cannot expect for my thoughts to mimic things that are pure and holy if I am filling my mind with the opposite material.

If you are looking to find spiritual strength and hope, it does not make sense to try to find it in a broken world. And yet, we do it all the time. "Let them alone; they are blind guides. And if the blind lead the blind, both will fall into a pit" (Matthew 15:14). We love to hear and watch things we can relate to, because they help us not to feel alone and alienated.

The problem comes when we shift unconsciously from simply relating to a song to emulating or accepting it. That is why the Bible teaches us to focus on "whatever is true, whatever is honorable, whatever is just, whatever is pure, whatever is lovely, whatever is commendable, if there is any excellence, if there is anything worthy of praise, think about these things" (Philippians 4:8). The apostle Paul knew the enemy would try to rob people of being able to know God and stay in His peace by keeping them in the position of feeling sorry for themselves.

Our emotions do not help, because, as the saying goes, misery loves company. The human mind loves to replay a bad thought and then find comfort in discovering others who feel the same way it does. As bad company corrupts good character, a bad thought that plays over and over corrupts your peace.

God used music to save my life, but because I had no grounding in God and no knowledge of His truth, I allowed the world to become my teacher. My love affair with music started off innocently, but as I delved into the world of broken souls who were using fame and money to fill their voids, my void, which could only be filled by God, became filled superficially with entertainment. I developed a hunger for success and fame, and I was indoctrinated in the things I needed to do to attain those things. Self-indulgence seems woven into what we are taught in America, but as with every other selfish desire, success and fame cannot satisfy us.

What are some other ways besides music that we can fill ourselves with good things? We can listen to the Word of God. We can keep a journal of good memories and put some reminders of those memories on Post-it notes and place them around our homes. We can watch wholesome movies or have stimulating conversations. When you wake up in the morning, before grabbing your phone and seeing the latest headline, take some time to begin your day in gratitude. Thank God for all that He has done. Thank Him for another day of life, for the shelter you have and anything that will keep you focused on your blessings rather than on what you lack. That will give you a good start.

As you go throughout your day, make the choice to refrain from entertaining negativity of any kind. You do not have to answer the phone or go to lunch with your gossiping co-worker, relative or neighbor. Keep yourself and your environment clear from things that will invite negativity into your world. Rather than scrolling through social media at night, put on worship music and let it play throughout your home. Grab your Bible and read from the book of Proverbs, which gives practical wisdom on how to stay blessed. I could go on and on. We really have many tools and resources at our disposal to stay encouraged, but we have to use them.

Our goal should always be to listen to God and His call. Jesus said, "My sheep hear my voice, and I know them, and they follow me" (John 10:27). He is the great shepherd, and His followers are His sheep. We will not hear His call if we are distracted by the noise of this world.

What Do I See?

1. What has God used in your life to help you get out of depression or suicidal thoughts?
2. What are some examples of times when entertainment influenced you?
3. What effects do you see from these influences? Have you been negatively inspired?

What Can I Learn?

- The enemy's tactics are all the same, and he sends things your way continually to fulfill his mission to steal, kill and destroy.
- An attack of suicidal thoughts can have a root of unresolved pain, unforgiveness or anger. Give your pain to God and allow Him to heal your brokenness.
- What we invest our time in, listen to and watch become the things we worship.

- The very thing God uses to help us can become a distraction that is used by the enemy to lead us astray.
- Do not look to broken people to help you heal from your brokenness. Only God can make you truly whole.
- What you dwell on and replay will affect how you feel. Focus on things that are praiseworthy, and remain in God's peace.

Scriptures for Meditation

Psalm 118:17 KJV
I shall not die, but live, and declare the works of the LORD.

Proverbs 3:5–6
Trust in the LORD with all your heart, and do not lean on your own understanding. In all your ways acknowledge him, and he will make straight your paths.

Philippians 4:8
Finally, brothers, whatever is true, whatever is honorable, whatever is just, whatever is pure, whatever is lovely, whatever is commendable, if there is any excellence, if there is anything worthy of praise, think about these things.

Colossians 2:8
See to it that no one takes you captive by philosophy and empty deceit, according to human tradition, according to the elemental spirits of the world, and not according to Christ.

John 10:27
My sheep hear my voice, and I know them, and they follow me.

Prayer and Declaration

Father God, in the name of Jesus I come to You, acknowledging You for who You are. You alone can take a broken vessel and make it whole. You are the giver of life. You breathe into each and every one of Your children, giving us purpose in this life. Lord, I pray that You would destroy every attack of the enemy over my life. Please give me the will to live and not die so that I can declare Your goodness to everyone I encounter. Deliver me from thoughts of hopelessness and suicide. Thank You for the times that You have saved my life. Help me not to idolize the things of this world or to become distracted by them. Jesus, take Your rightful place in my heart. I trust You, even when the lies of the enemy come. I choose to stand on Your truth about me and my destiny. Destroy every demonic attack that tries to make me forfeit Your plans in my life. Saturate me with Your Holy Spirit so that Your peace can reign in my being, and please enable me to hear Your voice so that I can live this life to the fullest. In Jesus' name, Amen.

5

Sex: Evil or of God?

Before we are old enough to understand fully what sex is, Satan has already begun to create a false definition in our minds about what it is and what its purpose is. This form of passion is a gift from God for us to use for our enjoyment and to populate the world. Satan, however, has taken it and perverted it. His interference has made sex hard for people to understand or talk about. If we are not taught the true purpose of sex, the enemy wins.

Desire is a real thing that he uses against you. Sexual perversion serves as a hook in your flesh, opening a portal that is hard to overcome by yourself. Even Christians can find themselves under the enemy's influence. In this chapter, I will discuss God's purpose for sex, the doors and traps to avoid and how we can find freedom from this stronghold together.

Appetites Awaken

As I began to grow and the world of entertainment was revealed to me, my appetite for the things of the flesh also grew. I became exposed to adult content at a really young age. A relative showed me how to unblock the adult content channel. I, in turn, showed all of my friends, both male and female. We, of course, wanted to emulate the things we saw. While I discovered that I was not attracted to the same sex, that fact did not stop me from indulging in the pleasures I received. It did not matter from whom those pleasures came.

Fortunately, I knew enough to realize I did not want to go all the way until I was older. Unfortunately, growing up in an oversexualized environment opened up a can of worms in my life. Even today, if I am not intentional about safeguarding myself in my private time, I feel the enemy trying to use this temptation against me.

One of the reasons that sexual perversion is a tough battle is because it causes such internal conflict. When you are exposed to the pleasure of the flesh as a child, you know that the act is bringing pleasure; however, you also know that something is not right and that you should not be doing it. Because it feels good, the enemy uses it to lure you in.

I often tell my friends and family members who are raising kids that if they do not educate their children about the purpose and origin of sex from the Bible, then the world and its perverted morals will teach their children about their sexuality. The next generation will have the same struggles that previous generations have had. There are mature Christians today who still struggle with this because Satan has controlled them in this area. He has created a false image of what God made for our pleasure.

There is a very interesting—and at the same time disturbing—passage in the Bible that talks about how the spiritual realm intersects with the natural realm when it comes to sex. Rebel spirits who were labeled sons of God and known as Nephilim had sex with human women to further pervert the earth and infect generations of people. Genesis shares the account of this cross contamination and how God felt about it.

> When people had spread all over the world, and daughters were being born, some of the heavenly beings saw that these young women were beautiful, so they took the ones they liked. Then the LORD said, "I will not allow people to live forever; they are mortal. From now on they will live no longer than 120 years." In those days, and even later, there were giants on the earth who were descendants of human women and the heavenly beings. They were the great heroes and famous men of long ago. When the LORD saw how wicked everyone on earth was and how evil their thoughts were all the time, he was sorry that he had ever made them and put them on the earth.
>
> Genesis 6:1–6 GNT

Fortunately for us, that lineage was wiped out. And yet, how do we in the here and now prevent the enemy from infecting our sexuality? Paul tells us that we should "Walk by the Spirit, and you will not gratify the desires of the flesh" (Galatians 5:16). I understand how difficult that is, though, when we are bombarded with over-sexualized content and imagery everywhere we turn.

A good friend of mine, Joe Battaglia, has been in marketing for many years. He shares a story about the time he took his daughter shopping at a famous brand-name store. Everywhere he turned there were billboards with half-naked people on them. Because of his background in marketing he knew that every billboard was intentional. He was appalled that a store selling clothing would feature images of people who barely had clothes on.

Those were the types of images that made me want to walk around half-dressed all the time. I showed my midriff every chance I could. I had no idea what message I was sending to everyone around me. I wanted to be as pretty as what I saw on TV. Since all of my music and movie heroes were selling their sensuality, I wanted to flaunt mine as well.

I am very thankful I was never abused sexually, but sadly I was sexually harassed as a child and preteen by several distant family members. A few were adults with sick pedophilia fantasies. What I did not know at the time was that every premature sexual experience I had was shaping the way I would think about sex.

The adults never talked to me about it, so I knew that it was something that had to be a secret. And because of what I watched on cable, I thought it was something that should happen with multiple partners, both male and female, friend or family. My view was distorted terribly. Never once did I think sex was something created for us by God. In fact, since I saw all of the priests and nuns within the Catholic Church living out a vow of celibacy, I thought that sex was condemned by the church. All of that made the desire of my flesh scream louder for pleasure, and it created rebellion in me.

God Made Sex

What the enemy does not want us to know is that when sex is not distorted, it is a pure and holy act created by God between a man and a woman in marriage. When God made Adam and Eve, He told them to "be fruitful and multiply and fill the earth" (Genesis 1:28). He wanted them to be free to procreate. It was not until the enemy deceived them into eating the fruit in the garden that they noticed their nakedness. Perverting sex is exactly what Satan does. This perverted view of sex makes us feel as if we should partake of it in secret and with shame. If we associate shame with sex, we are not able to experience freedom in marriage. How many times have you heard the saying that sex dies once someone is married? Now ask yourself, who would want you to think that? Paul says that the exact opposite is true.

> The husband should give to his wife her conjugal rights, and likewise the wife to her husband. For the wife does not have authority over her own body, but the husband does. Likewise the husband does not have authority over his own body, but the wife does. Do not deprive one another, except perhaps by agreement for a limited time, that you may devote yourselves to prayer; but then come together again, so that Satan may not tempt you because of your lack of self-control.
>
> 1 Corinthians 7:3–5

God led the apostle Paul to help believers know that they should indulge in a sexual relationship with their spouse. If they do not, the enemy is waiting to step between them to pervert and destroy. King Solomon talked often about the act of sex between a husband and a wife and how the two should come together as one. Chapter four of Song of Solomon takes the reader into the bedroom of King Solomon and his bride right after their wedding. He begins by expressing his admiration for her and every detail of her body. He talks about her scent and her tongue, and he compares her to a garden whose fountain is flowing. In chapter seven of that book, the heat turns up as the couple both talk about a night of lovemaking.

When writing about the sanctity of a husband and wife's bedroom time, the author of Hebrews says, "Let marriage be held in honor among all, and let the marriage bed be undefiled" (13:4). Why would sex be something exclusively for marriage? Is it because God is some cruel dictator who does not want His kids to have fun and indulge in things that feel good? That is not it at all. God knows what is best for us, and any good father warns his children of things that are dangerous for them. Adultery, fornication and self-indulgence can be detrimental to your growth.

When people have sex with someone other than the one with whom they will spend their life forever, a piece of them is given to that person. Look at it as a plant. A plant potted in dirt begins to spread its roots in that specific pot. That, in turn, reflects in the plant's personal growth. In this illustration, the pot is a partner with whom you, the plant, have made an intimate connection. Things are great for a time, but because there was no lifelong commitment, you break up eventually and move on. You, the plant, are then uprooted and planted somewhere else, leaving some of your roots in the last pot. You may be in new soil, but some of your roots were left behind. What do you think will happen if you continually uproot yourself in that pattern? Eventually, all of your roots will be left in various pots, and your plant will wither and die.

Sure, we have the freedom to choose to sleep around and have various partners. Each time that we do, however, those connections cause soul ties that harm us. This lifestyle is really not worth the internal damage it causes. God knows this, so He designed a road map for us in His Word to help us avoid that. The apostle Paul speaks about this.

> Do you not know that your bodies are members of Christ? Shall I then take the members of Christ and make them members of a prostitute? Never! Or do you not know that he who is joined to a prostitute becomes one body with her? For, as it is written, "The two will become one flesh." But he who is joined to the Lord becomes one spirit with him. Flee from sexual immorality. Every other sin a person commits is outside the body, but the sexually immoral person sins against his own body.
>
> 1 Corinthians 6:15–18

There is a famous quote that says, "Sex is the biggest nothing of all time."[1] That is one of the biggest deceptions of all time. Going from one partner to another diminishes your self-worth. As the Scripture above says, sexual immorality is a sin we commit against ourselves. God designed marriage as a union that creates oneness: one in heart, one in spirit and one in flesh. Everyone has a yearning for that pure connection, whether they admit it or not. Unless, of course, God gives them a special grace to devote themselves only to God and His work.

Even before I knew God, I felt dirty and guilty when I explored my sexuality outside of the purity that God intended. As I came to know Jesus and submitted my sexual appetite to

1. Leslie Halliwell, *Halliwell's Filmgoer's Companion: Incorporating the Filmgoer's Book of Quotes and Halliwell's Movie Quiz* (New York: Harper Perennial), 714.

Him, I found the times that I was tempted most were when I had an inner sadness that I had not addressed. Loneliness, grief or self-pity served as doors for the enemy to convince me that I needed to find comfort somehow, whether through pornography or a partner.

That kind of comfort is an illusion, however. Even if you indulge in those acts, the situations that caused your sadness do not vanish magically. Instead, you must see those attacks as signals that you need help. God is the one who can see deep into our hearts and can help us. In the book *The World, the Flesh, and Father Smith*, Bruce Marshall agrees with this notion. He says, "The young man who rings the bell at the brothel is unconsciously looking for God."[2] Wanting to indulge carelessly in your sexual appetite is a sign that your heart is searching for greater meaning. Believe me, sex cannot fill that void.

What can you do to overcome the temptations of the flesh? I did not learn these lessons until I surrendered my life to God—but, man, I sure wish I had known these things as a child. The only thing that kept me from having sexual intercourse in my preteens and early teens was the fact that my mom always told me that she had waited until marriage to have sex. Whether it was true or not was irrelevant. I believed her, and I felt as if I should wait as well. I did wait to have sex longer than most of my peers, but unfortunately, I caved in to the temptations.

Sexual connections form soul ties. Imagine that you have your own baggage. When you sleep with someone who is not your spouse, that connection ties you to his or her body

2. Bruce Marshall, *The World, The Flesh and Father Smith* (State College, Pennsylvania: Image Books, 1957), 114.

as well as to his or her baggage. It was not God's intention that you carry that baggage, but when you have sex with others, you form spiritual ties with them. Those connections must be broken.

Believe me, I experienced the regret of those decisions when I got married and became one with my husband. I felt that I had robbed him of the most precious part of me. I also felt as if I had to erase the memories of my past that wanted to enter into our bedroom and destroy my sex life with the one for whom it was intended. I had to purge myself of everything from my past and pray that the Lord would deliver me from the memories so that I could enjoy the freedom of married sex.

If you are single, please trust me. Work on all this before you go into marriage. The only soul you want to be tied to is your husband or wife. I have seen it firsthand. God can help us live a pure life if we are serious about it. In my singleness, I realized how true this Bible verse is:

> No temptation has overtaken you that is not common to man. God is faithful, and he will not let you be tempted beyond your ability, but with the temptation he will also provide the way of escape, that you may be able to endure it.
>
> 1 Corinthians 10:13

God makes a way for us to escape sexual sin, but we have to want to take the escape route. Whether it is through online software programs that help block pornography or by having people hold you accountable, there are resources to help you. Use them and keep your purity. One good way to fight the spirit of lust in your life is to fill your mind and heart with the Word of God. Study His ways. There is no better way to distract yourself from temptation than by staying focused on God and the call that He has placed on your life.

I often hear that men are the ones who battle perversion most, but I do not believe that. We are all being assaulted constantly by sexual symbolism, and the last time that I checked, both men and women were guilty of falling into this sin. The good news is that we do not have to buy into everything this world offers us. Once we commit our lives to Christ we can put on His nature and turn away from sin, because we are no longer of this world. We have a greater purpose.

If we set our affections on Him and close any doors the enemy might have into our lives, we make it harder for that temptation to seep in. If you think about it, when are people prone to cheat on their partners? When they feel lonely or neglected. When do people watch pornography or engage in self-indulgence? When they are alone or everyone else is off to bed. The goal is to be so full of God that we need not turn to what the enemy is offering us.

I will share this example to help you understand better. Let's say you invite someone you really admire to come over and spend the weekend with you. You clean the house, you prepare their favorite meal, you serve them, and you make sure that they feel at home in your presence. You become so engulfed in your guest of honor that you rarely look at your phone. You keep bathroom breaks to a minimum because you want to enjoy every moment with them.

What if we treated God that way? What if we spent our lives living to host the greatest hero of all? The loneliness, helplessness, neglect and whatever else the enemy uses to lull us into sin would not work because we would be too busy entertaining our Master. If you find yourself bored, get in the Word or watch a Christian film or a sermon. Do not bring the phone to bed with you. Leave it far away. You have to safeguard your sexuality because the enemy is always looking to creep in and tempt you.

Another way to avoid allowing sexual imagery to seep into your spirit is to bounce your eyes. You cannot allow the enemy to captivate your attention. If you see something risky, look the other way—bounce your eyes. If you stare or give temptation a second glance, you are more likely to entertain the evil. That is how ties can form, especially for people who are stimulated visually.

I am a part of a group of girls who hold each other accountable. We differ in age and race, some are single, some are married, but in this group, we share our battles honestly. We realized this is not only a single person's battle—it is an every-person battle. A tool that came up in one of our many conversations was the acronym H.A.L.T. The letters stand for Hungry, Angry, Lonely and Tired. I first heard this example from Dr. Charles Stanley, who said people are most tempted by Satan when they are in one or more of the aforementioned states.[3] All of my girlfriends found this to be true. If you find yourself feeling weakened by the enemy, you should not only check your spiritual health, but you should check your physical health as well. Do something to help yourself flee from the inducement.

Sexuality is a powerful force. When we do not value it the way God designed it to be in marriage, we can get tricked

3. Dr. Charles Stanley, "Moments of Weakness," *In Touch Daily Devotional*, June 25, 2007, https://www.oneplace.com/devotionals/in-touch-with-charles -stanley/in-touch-june-25-2007-11545170.html.

into a life of secrecy. The moment lust was awakened in me as a child I began living a double life. I could not be honest with my loved ones about it because it was such a taboo topic. Furthermore, when distant relatives violated me sexually as a child, I did not think I could say anything to anyone. As I got older, I had no one from whom I could seek advice.

The saying used in the world of addiction recovery is that we are only as sick as our secrets.[4] Shame and guilt bring torment. Our best defense against this, however, is exposing our battles and pursuing freedom. There is another slogan used in a campaign against pornography that states that porn kills love.[5] Unless you have battled sexual sin yourself, you do not really understand this slogan.

God, however, revealed the meaning of it to me when I asked Him about it. Lust of the flesh is a sin against your body. The more we indulge it, the more shame and guilt we feel until the point that we numb the conviction altogether. This numbness is what kills true intimacy. You begin to see people as objects of pleasure and not as people who have a purpose.

Intimacy goes beyond a physical connection, and it happens when you allow someone into the depths of who you are. If sex is the only goal, then true closeness will never be established.

Before you move on to the next chapter, take some time to examine the things in your life that might provide an open door to the enemy in his pursuit of perverting your sexuality.

4. Natalie Baker, "We're Only as Sick as Our Secrets," Recovery.org, January 30, 2017, https://www.recovery.org/were-only-as-sick-as-our-secrets/.
5. "How Porn Kills Love," Fight the New Drug, May 4, 2017, https://fight thenewdrug.org/how-porn-kills-love/.

What Do I See?

1. What did the family environment you grew up in teach you about sexuality and marriage?
2. What are some of the patterns that led to the enemy tempting you to fall into sexual sin?
3. What are some of the things you can do to safeguard yourself from indulging in self-pleasure, fornication or adultery?
4. What effect has perversion had on your life or those around you?

What Can I Learn?

- God created sex, but the enemy has perverted it, using entertainment and media to rob people of its true purpose.
- Sex was made for a man and woman in the confines of marriage to enjoy and to populate the earth.
- The enemy attaches shame and guilt to sexuality as a way of keeping people in bondage to it.
- Sex outside of marriage creates soul ties that must be broken.
- God provides a way for His people to combat the temptations of the world through the Holy Spirit, the Bible, computer/phone filtering programs, etc.
- Be honest with people you trust who will keep you accountable.

- There is freedom from secret sin, such as pornography and lust, but you have to expose it and allow God to deliver you.

Scriptures for Meditation

Hebrews 13:4
Let marriage be held in honor among all, and let the marriage bed be undefiled, for God will judge the sexually immoral and adulterous.

1 Corinthians 7:2
But because of the temptation to sexual immorality, each man should have his own wife and each woman her own husband.

1 Thessalonians 4:3–5
For this is the will of God, your sanctification: that you abstain from sexual immorality; that each one of you know how to control his own body in holiness and honor, not in the passion of lust like the Gentiles who do not know God.

Proverbs 6:32
He who commits adultery lacks sense; he who does it destroys himself.

Prayer and Declaration

Father God, in the name of Jesus I come to You to commit the members of my body to You. Lord, I desire to be holy, pure and to live a life of self-control. Help me to guard my eyes and my spirit from lust, perversion and sexual sin. Lord, break every generational understanding of sexual corruption. Help me to see that sex is made by You for a husband and wife to enjoy. Break off any soul ties I created from past relationships and purify me for You and my (future) spouse. Remove every distortion of sex that I have or was taught and rewrite the definition of sexuality for me. Lord, I submit myself to You. Wash me clean and make me whole. In Jesus' name, Amen.

6

Demons of Distraction

People tend to idolize the blessings in their lives, including careers, education, possessions, dreams and even family members. The enemy loves to use our blessings as deterrents. He knows he has an open door to our lives once we get consumed by what we do or have. He then makes it his business to keep us distracted by those things.

I felt as if my life was so rough that I had to go out and become a famous star, so I ran straight into the entertainment industry. I hoped that everything would change. Boy, was I wrong! Although I had good intentions, I would soon be taken off any good path I had been on. I ended up heading toward a path of self-indulgence and idolatry without even realizing that my course had changed.

In this chapter you will discover how easy it is to become distracted when your focus is not on God and His purposes for your life. You will be able to identify the enemy's tricks concerning using what we love and how he makes those things idols to us, which then draw us away from God. You will also learn the pitfalls to avoid when your dreams begin to come true.

Modern Idolatry

My desire to sing and help people through music continued to increase, as did the tension in my home; therefore, I continued to pursue a way out. One day, while I was still in my very early teens, my big break in the music industry came. I had spent years singing everywhere I could, I had worked with different managers and I had even been in a girl group, but each scenario proved to be a big scam. Every loss left me feeling disenchanted. Even still, those bad experiences did not stop me from longing to be a star. I believe God gave me the desires of my heart so that I could see that apart from Him not even those things that I was dreaming about fulfilled me.

Everything changed for me after a day of shopping with my mom. We hailed a cab from the supermarket parking lot, loaded our groceries (or what Puerto Ricans would call *compra*) and headed home. If you know me, you know I do not sit quietly for long without bursting into song, and this was the case that day. I began singing along to the radio. As we approached my home the cab driver started to ask questions about my talent. Before I knew it, I was handing him a demo recording of my songs. He promised to give it to one of his famous clients who he knew from his time driving a limo.

To my surprise, I received a call a few weeks later that would change my life forever. An established manager was on the line and, in her words, she felt compelled to call me after her limo driver had handed her my demo. After that phone call, everything moved very quickly. My dreams were becoming a reality as I found myself singing in mega-studios and working on music with established writers and producers.

At first, my goals were to make music to help other young girls find comfort and to be someone they could relate to, but as soon as I got to work in the studio, I was being told what I needed to succeed. My big mission in life changed quickly. When you are offered what you always have dreamed of, it is important that you stick to your convictions. Although I thought that I was a tough girl from Brooklyn who was not going to let anyone change me, I caved when the world offered me what I had always wanted. Without hesitation, I gave in to what the studio executives thought would be best for me. I figured that they were the experts, so I should follow their lead.

Have you ever received the promotion you were waiting desperately for but then realized that it was nothing like what you had expected, because the job required you to conform to what your superiors demanded of you? Well, that is what happened to me, and that is how my career became an idol to me.

It reminds me of the conversation the serpent had with Eve in the Garden of Eden. She knew that her place in the garden was to live free and serve God, but once she started wandering around and was introduced to something other than what her initial purpose was, she went astray. I find that when we go astray life becomes unnecessarily harder for us—as it also did for Adam and Eve. "The LORD God sent him out from the garden of Eden to work the ground from which he was taken" (Genesis 3:23). This verse is written after Adam went amiss and allowed the enemy to distort the blessing of God.

Adam and Eve's desire for the knowledge of good and evil became something that they wanted more than everything God had promised them in the garden. That form of idolatry is the reason we all live in a fallen world. Before the Fall, heaven and earth intersected in the garden. Adam and Eve had all they could have wanted, but the serpent knew that if he could make them lust for things they did not have, they would soon think about those things more than what God had already given them.

Taste-the-Fruit Moments

Our own taste-the-fruit moments in life will always lead us down a path for which we did not set out. As for me, going into the music industry in my early teens was my way out of the life that I was running away from. I have found that when boundaries are gone, most of us end up discovering what we are really made of. Let's face it, a life without rules or major responsibilities is appealing to our flesh.

The secular music industry at that time was exactly what people called it: the devil's playground. I was ambushed easily because I went into that battleground without any armor on. Ambition, and not God, was my focus. It did not matter how spiritual I was, just as it does not matter how old or young you are. Once you are initiated into that world you are fair game. It is as if you have a target on you that says, "Hey, devil, come get me." That is what happens to us all when we move ahead with our careers, jobs and daily tasks without keeping God front and center.

I would like to take a closer look at exactly what it looks like to put on your spiritual armor. The book of Ephesians breaks it down for us.

> Therefore take up the whole armor of God, that you may be able to withstand in the evil day, and having done all, to stand firm. Stand therefore, having fastened on the belt of truth, and having put on the breastplate of righteousness, and, as shoes for your feet, having put on the readiness given by the gospel of peace. In all circumstances take up the shield of faith, with which you can extinguish all the flaming darts of the evil one; and take the helmet of salvation, and the sword of the Spirit, which is the word of God, praying at all times in the Spirit, with all prayer and supplication.
>
> Ephesians 6:13–18

This means we have to make sure that when we are out in the world we are locked and loaded in the spirit. The apostle Paul did not write this chapter for people who are going out to battle in a physical war. He wrote it for everyday Christians who are trying to live better lives and who are being assaulted constantly by the spiritual lure of this world that is hoping to use our dreams and goals to guide us away from God.

The Belt of Truth

Putting on your spiritual armor is very instrumental in helping you avoid falling into idolatry. Had I known the truth about my identity and worth, I would not have become obsessed with my image. When the industry told me I still had baby fat and I needed to lose weight—even though I weighed only 115 pounds and was fifteen years old—I shifted my focus. Before their influence, I had wanted to help people through my music. After their influence, I wanted to make the girls want to be me and make the guys want to be with me. Had I known the truth about my identity, I would not have shifted my focus.

Creating a sexy image was something I was groomed constantly to do as a young teenager in the industry. And believe me, the words that the adults around me used were not as PG as I just phrased them. Did you have a similar experience within your circle of friends? Did you go into a situation with positive intentions but were distracted by the demands or suggestions of the world around you?

The Bible suggests that we wear truth as a belt that supports us. If you do not know the truth, however, you cannot wear it as a belt. What is truth? Jesus said, "I am the way, and the truth, and the life. No one comes to the Father except through me" (John 14:6). Later, in John 16:13, Jesus calls the Holy Spirit the "Spirit of truth" and says, "He will guide you into all the truth." But if Jesus is the truth and His Holy Spirit is also called truth, then how can the human mind comprehend truth?

Well, Jesus gives us the answer while He is praying to God the Father. "Sanctify them in the truth; your word is truth" (John 17:17). It can be really hard to go into spiritual warfare and fight off the world's system that is beckoning us to conform to its way of thinking. But if we recondition ourselves with God's Word, then we are not as susceptible to life's idols.

I was in bondage to the entertainment industry for years. I lost my way and purpose, because I did everything through the lens of this world. I did not know the truth about myself in God, I did not realize that I was not of this world, nor did I know that I did not have to follow the culture of the world. Years later when my eyes were opened to the truth, I saw the impact of what Jesus meant when He said, "And you will know the truth, and the truth will set you free" (John 8:32). Be sure that you to go into every part of your world wearing the truth of God around you as your support. You do not want to fall for the lusts of the world and suffer the consequences as I did.

Breastplate of Righteousness

Righteousness is such a serious word. Because of what I experienced and my lack of knowledge of God, I should not have had an inkling of being righteous; however, that is one thing my father instilled in me. It was important to him that he taught me character, morals and a sense of self-respect, even if he did not always exhibit those things himself. Paul teaches that for our sake God made Jesus to be sin who knew no sin, "so that in him we might become the righteousness of God" (2 Corinthians 5:21). Although I tried to be righteous, I did not understand what that meant.

Let me explain. Unfortunately, I am one of a number of women who say, "Me Too."[6] I was sexually harassed by those in power over me. I was only a teenager, but that did not stop the predators of the entertainment industry from making advances at me or over-sexualizing many of our conversations to manipulate me into their grasp. The enemy knew

6. Tarana Burke, "History and Inception," *Me Too*, 2020, https://metoomvmt.org/get-to-know-us/history-inception/.

I was a prime candidate for going astray because of what I had been through, and because I wanted desperately to become famous. Wanting fame is a demonic ambition that is spearheaded by the evil one.

Thankfully, my dad's deposits of character and morals in my life gave me a sense of self-respect. Those seeds of righteousness caused me to fight off many of my assailants before anything went too far. I was once in a studio booth in front of a huge pop producer, singing a song I had written. I had my eyes closed, as I did when I sang, when I felt a man standing behind me breathing on my neck and rubbing himself against me. That "big shot" producer had snuck into the recording booth with me.

Without thinking twice, I clenched my fist and swung under the belt. I was terrified and wondered what would happen next. He said it was simply a joke, and he left the room. Had I not been told by my dad that I should respect myself, I might have been too afraid or intimidated to react the way that I did. I did not know God's Word or His standard of righteousness, but my godly moral compass must have picked up on a signal, because I knew I could not stand for being some rich man's object. To be clear, I know that I must have been protected divinely, because that same scenario could have ended very differently if the producer had fought back.

Due to my obsession with becoming famous, I put myself in dangerous positions many times. I barely escaped from getting trapped into some dark and twisted scenarios with other celebrities and rock stars, both male and female. Honestly, there were even times I gave in to some advances. I was young, and I found it fascinating that older, successful men could be interested in me. By the grace of God, though, I never let the advances go further than a kiss.

Looking back, I see that those advances were pedophilia and abuse of power. Those in authority were using their positions over me to coerce me into giving them what they wanted. When there are idols in our life, the enemy uses them to control us. He takes intimidation, status and abuse of authority to try to beat us into submission. We know, however, that Jesus has overcome this world. We do not have to be afraid of people who try to lord their power over us.

What would it have looked like in these scenarios if I had known my identity in Christ? How would wearing the breastplate of righteousness have changed my position? I believe that I would have left situations such as these and reported the sexual harassment and brought these people to justice. Or, maybe I would not have been in those situations in the first place.

When we do not have a proper understanding of sin, we do not have a proper understanding of righteousness. "Blessed are they who observe justice, who do righteousness at all times" (Psalm 106:3). Sure, this comes with the threat of losing some relationships. For some, it might mean even losing their careers. But the Bible is clear that people who suffer for righteousness will be taken care of by God. "If you should suffer for righteousness' sake, you will be blessed. Have no fear of them, nor be troubled" (1 Peter 3:14).

You will find that even in the Church there is unrighteousness. Jesus warned us when He said, "Unless your righteousness exceeds that of the scribes and Pharisees, you will never enter the kingdom of heaven" (Matthew 5:20). We must know what sin and righteousness are according to the standards of the

Bible. Even things that are seemingly good can become idols to us. We live in a world that calls evil good and good evil, and we have an enemy who will use all things against us.

Shoes of Peace

Oh, how I wish I had known peace during this stage of my life. I knew how to fight to survive and how to fight for my worldly reputation, but I did not know peace. Chaos and recklessness were a part of me. This chaos was even present when I flew to Hollywood and got offered my record deal. I walked into the label with my bad girl persona and pretty much told them that if they knew what was good for them, they would sign me to a deal and give me all of my demands. Oddly enough, this label that was associated with a mega enterprise aimed at entertaining children welcomed me and all of my destructive behavior. I invited anarchy into my life, and I bullied or ran over anyone who I felt was in my way.

I had no concept of peace until I became an adult and learned about the Prince of Peace. It was only then that I learned what peace felt like by being in the presence of God. I had no idea that I could walk in peace even as the world around me came crashing down. I had no idea of the security that came with peace. I tried, instead, to drown out my inner turmoil with music, which became my saving grace. Music brought temporary happiness to me, but not the lasting joy that I needed to feel secure. Perhaps I experienced moments of peace, but they were always short-lived and overshadowed by the madness that surrounded me. The enemy also fueled that chaos every chance he could.

Jesus made it clear that in the world we will have tribulation. He also assured us that we could have peace in Him because He overcame the world (see John 16:33). To experience that peace, however, you cannot be distracted by the world. What does the peace of God look or feel like? Well, Jesus shared about it in the book of John when He explained that it is incomprehensible to us because it is not a peace that the world offers. His peace surpasses understanding. "Peace I leave with you; my peace I give to you. Not as the world gives do I give to you. Let not your hearts be troubled, neither let them be afraid" (John 14:27). We see from this statement that there is no fear when we experience God's peace.

You can forget about my having been peaceful with others at this stage of my life. I was taught to always look people in the eye, and if anyone ever looked at me wrong, I was to confront them. Further, I was told that if I ever got into a fight, I was to hit the other person until I saw blood. I was a child of the world and trouble pursued me. I cannot even count the number of fights, with both males and females, I got into from the age of seven to seventeen. What I did not know at the time was that blessings follow people who pursue peace with others. "Blessed are the peacemakers, for they shall be called sons of God" (Matthew 5:9).

The Bible says clearly that we should seek and pursue peace. The world is nothing but confusing and chaotic without God's peace resting on it. It is not always going to be easy practicing peace—such as with a co-worker who gets on your nerves or with a family member who knows how to push the right button—but walking in peace with others is important for our maturity. Getting things my way had become an idol in my life, and the disorder that came when

I did not get things my way was what kept me in a perpetual state of anger.

I wish it had not taken me as long to realize that pursuing peace was the answer that I desired, even if that meant laying down my wants and needs. Walking out peace with my dad years later completely changed my family. Today we all work actively to put the other person first and to preserve that peace, both internally and externally, with others. Once my life changed and everyone around me saw that I no longer reacted to chaos with more chaos, they were forced to reconsider their own reactions. My consistent approach to follow peace with my loved ones became one of the biggest examples for my family. My fists turned into hugs, and my curse words turned into repentance. This outcome was all because of the inner work of serenity that God had done in my heart. Now I can say gratefully that my parents and siblings all live to pursue peace in their own lives.

Shield of Faith

I love that the Bible describes faith as our shield of protection, because it really is! As a child, I had faith that I could do anything. I believe it is even the reason I attained my dreams at such an early age. I mean, come on. I was discovered singing in a New York City taxi, I flew across the country to Hollywood and I was offered a record deal on the spot. Talent plays a minor factor in that. I believe it was my childlike faith that broke down all of the barriers of impossibility that came with being a Latina from the ghetto of New York.

Scripture talks about childlike faith and how it is linked to experiencing the Kingdom of God. "Without faith it is impossible to please him" (Hebrews 11:6). Jesus challenged His followers to have faith in God to do anything.

> "Have faith in God. Truly, I say to you, whoever says to this mountain, 'Be taken up and thrown into the sea,' and does not doubt in his heart, but believes that what he says will come to pass, it will be done for him. Therefore I tell you, whatever you ask in prayer, believe that you have received it, and it will be yours."
>
> Mark 11:22–24

In order to fight off idolatry, you have to put your faith in the right thing. Idols in our lives, such as money, status or people, reveal that our faith is in things other than God.

The faith that I had in myself and in the gift that God had given me to sing paved the way for me. When I got up on stage, whether it was in an arena, a mall, an outdoor stadium or a nightclub, I wanted the audience to understand that God was the reason that I had made it out of the hood and into Hollywood. Have you ever experienced being positive and sure that God was leading your path, but when you got what you prayed for, things changed? Well, I did. I had made it. I was young, using my talents, making money, traveling the world and hanging out with celebrities, but my faith had shifted. What had once been faith in God and what He had given me to do had shifted to listening to everyone around me and what they thought I should do.

The Bible warns, "That your faith might not rest in the wisdom of men but in the power of God" (1 Corinthians 2:5). But because I had no godly guidance, I fell into the trap. The people who were guiding me enjoyed the power I gave them over my life and career. Because of this, the enemy influenced them to lead me further away from my true purpose in life. I learned what the real world was like through the lens of a deceptive industry in which everyone was trying to get something from me. I even led my friends, family and fans down that evil road with me. Because of my impressionable mind and ignorance, I put my faith in people. I allowed their goals for me to become idols. The Bible advises against this, saying, "Little children, keep yourselves from idols" (1 John 5:21).

During this phase of my life, I also fell deeply in love with my high school sweetheart. He was a "bad boy," and I was infatuated with him all throughout high school. Once my fame skyrocketed, so did my love for him. That combination of fame and infatuation built a tower of idolatry so tall that it knocked my purpose into the stratosphere. I was never more broken and lost than I was during this time. I turned into a people pleaser because I thought it would make my life better.

While in this relationship, I became a stereotypical pop star who did what I was told by my handlers. I had no idea that God had a plan for me. I did not have a faith in God, so while the people in the industry were dressing me and designing video and photo shoots that glorified the occult, I was entertaining a toxic relationship with my high school sweetheart, who was as broken as I was. I was living with him and watching the relationship start to model some of the behavior I had witnessed as a child. I now had more money, fame and company than ever, but my life was spiraling.

I am sure we all have had moments when we believed that what we do is who we are. Have you been there? Think about it. The first thing we usually tell people when talking about ourselves is what our occupation is, as if somehow that defines who we are. Even after we come to the knowledge of God, we tend to "humbly" brag of our accomplishments. In the book *Mere Christianity*, C. S. Lewis refers to pride as the great sin and says, "Pride leads to every other vice: it is the complete anti-God state of mind."[7] True faith in God is our shield against the pride of life and idolizing the things we do or are given. "Can we boast, then, that we have done anything to be accepted by God? No, because our acquittal is not based on obeying the law. It is based on faith" (Romans 3:27 NLT).

Task vs. Purpose

I will continue to talk about the importance of having spiritual armor on, specifically the helmet of salvation and the sword of the Spirit, in the next chapter, but I want to park here for a minute. Many people have a hard time laying down their idols because the enemy has made it seem as if it is too hard to do. He lies to us and makes us believe that the thing we idolize would fall apart if we let it go. We give in to these things because we are prioritizing the tasks of life before the purpose God has for our lives. Music was how God saved my life. I then realized I had a purpose to use music to help others. But before I could complete that purpose, the details and tasks that came with performing became more of a priority than my purpose.

While driving, if another driver cuts you off and you respond by honking your horn and yelling, you have allowed the task of driving to take the focus off of your purpose, which

7. C. S. Lewis, *Mere Christianity* (San Francisco: Harper One, 2009), 132.

is to be a representation of Christ even while on the road. Many times, I have allowed the task and responsibilities of my life to take precedence over my purpose. In turn, I robbed myself from being able to do what God created me to do. When we begin to shift our focus from the one who blesses to the blessing itself, from the giver to the gift, from the Creator to creation, then we begin to idolize those things. Every idol begins in the heart (see Ezekiel 14:4). God shares His glory with nothing and no one, and we cannot serve both.

> "You shall have no other gods before me. You shall not make for yourself a carved image, or any likeness of anything that is in heaven above, or that is in the earth beneath, or that is in the water under the earth. You shall not bow down to them or serve them, for I the Lord your God am a jealous God."
>
> Exodus 20:3–4

How do we navigate success or receiving the things for which we prayed? We need to keep Jesus at the center of it all. God wants us to be successful. The Bible talks about our gifts making way for us (see Proverbs 18:16) and bringing us before royalty (see Proverbs 22:29), but our boast should never be our accomplishments or those who helped us to accomplish them. The glory alone belongs to God, the one who makes a way for us.

The evil one will try to lead us into spiritual adultery, or he will demand that we give him the glory. This deception is what he has been doing since he was kicked out of heaven for trying to exalt himself over God. We must deflect any glory given to us, and we should make sure that we are a reflection of Christ. Also, we must be equipped fully in our spiritual armor. Remember that we are living in a world that is run by the enemy of our soul, and that enemy is baiting us constantly to serve creation rather than the Creator.

What Do I See?

1. What blessings and dreams have you allowed to become idols in your life (family, career or gifts)?
2. How can equipping yourself with spiritual armor keep you from falling into idolatry?
3. What blessings in your life came from having childlike faith? What things have distracted you from believing for more?
4. How can you make God the center of the blessings He has given you?

What Can I Learn?

- Chasing success, fame and wealth leads to idolatry.
- You must be fully equipped with your spiritual armor to withstand the attack of idolatry.
- Childlike faith opens impossible doors in your life, but the enemy will try to take your focus off of God.
- Pride is the breeding ground for more sin.
- God wants us to be successful, but then we are to humble ourselves and point the glory back to Him.
- We need to carry Jesus with us and be the reflection of God in a world that is led by another master.

Scriptures for Meditation

Matthew 6:24

"No one can serve two masters, for either he will hate the one and love the other, or he will be devoted to the one and despise the other. You cannot serve God and money."

Psalm 135:15–18

The idols of the nations are silver and gold, the work of human hands. They have mouths, but do not speak; they have eyes, but do not see; they have ears, but do not hear, nor is there any breath in their mouths. Those who make them become like them, so do all who trust in them.

Ephesians 6:13–18

Therefore take up the whole armor of God, that you may be able to withstand in the evil day, and having done all, to stand firm. Stand therefore, having fastened on the belt of truth, and having put on the breastplate of righteousness, and, as shoes for your feet, having put on the readiness given by the gospel of peace. In all circumstances take up the shield of faith, with which you can extinguish all the flaming darts of the evil one; and take the helmet of salvation, and the sword of the Spirit, which is the word of God, praying at all times in the Spirit, with all prayer and supplication.

1 Corinthians 10:14

Therefore, my beloved, flee from idolatry.

Prayer and Declaration

Thank You so much, God, for all that You give freely to me. Reveal to me anything in my life that I have put before You. God, I pray that You will help me not to worship the blessing, praise the gift or idolize the social status. May You alone be Lord and King in my life. Because You are the gift giver, the one who blesses, the one who promotes, the one who grants success, and the one who opens the doors that no man can shut. I pray that You would reveal any idols that I have in my heart. I lay those things down before You and cast them away. Have mercy on me for putting anything before You, and deliver me from the schemes of the enemy that try to lure me away from You. Father, I want You to take Your rightful place in my life and within my affections. May all glory be given to You alone, and may all that I do be for You and motivated by You. You alone are my greatest desire. May my life be a true reflection of that. I ask all of this in Jesus' name, Amen.

Baby Jeannie in an incubator

Mommy holding Jeannie

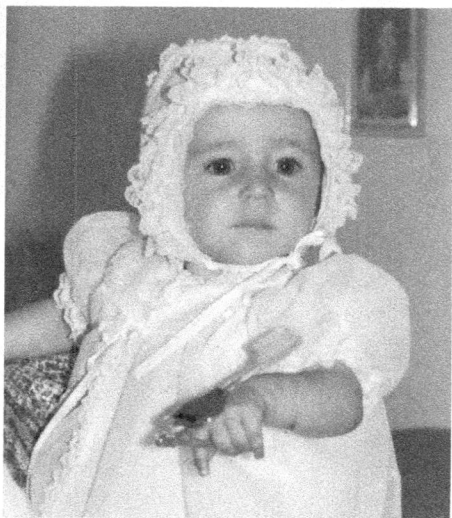

Infant baptism

My first communion

Adult baptism

After Sunday school with
Pastor Bill Wilson

On tour in Arizona 2006

In the studio

Height of pop
success, Webster
Hall NYC

Worshiping after
transformation
in Christ

Wedding day
12/27/2009

The Laws
(Rev. Renn and
Jeannie)

Ministering with
husband on TBN

7

God Wrestles for You

Some may never understand how real the spiritual battle for their soul is. Until I became a Christian, I did not realize how many times God had kept evil, danger and trouble away from me. It did not matter how far I strayed from Him—He was faithful to me. We may not be faithful, but He is. The enemy of our souls will pursue us to steal, kill and destroy our lives and purposes, but Jesus tells us specifically in His Word that we do not need to be worried, because He is greater than the evil of this world.

What we need to do, however, is not make it harder for ourselves by rejecting God and His divine love and protection. In this chapter, I will give you a glimpse of how the enemy beckons and tries to overtake us by using our thoughts and emotions. God, on the other hand, intervenes and helps us fight for our lives, for His purposes and for His destiny for us.

Success with No Peace

I now had everything I had ever dreamed of: a music career, what I thought was true love, and enough money to answer all the problems of life. Even still, I had no peace. After another big blow up in my home, I was left feeling numb and as if I should give up on everything, including my life. Fulfilling all of my goals, being accomplished or having hundreds of thousands of dollars in my bank account did not fill the deep void that I had.

When I was not in the studio or traveling, I was a student at Brooklyn High School of the Arts. After this latest fight in my home, I walked around school like a living zombie. I was depressed and suicidal because I could not understand why money, success or fame did not change my home and heart. The enemy had me believing that all hope was lost. God, however, would not leave me in that state. He sent a lifeline.

As I was entering history class, a peer of mine walked up to me and asked me randomly if I needed to go to church. We were distant friends at the time, so she could not have had any idea about how I was feeling. What she also had no way of knowing was that the night before I had told God that I needed to go to church, but that I felt as if could not go to my childhood church because I was afraid of the priest. I felt that he hated me and would lead me into a darker place. After she asked me that question, I gasped for air in complete shock. How on earth could God have communicated with her that specifically? God must have led her to me because He did not want the spirit of suicide to overtake me.

You Can Feel God

We see over and over in Scripture that God tells His people that He fights their battles and that they need not worry (see Deuteronomy 1:30; 3:22; 20:4; Exodus 14:14; Joshua 23:10). In that moment I was so weak that I felt paralyzed. God really did send me a raft in the middle of the ocean of my despair. The invitation was proof to me that something bigger than me was listening to my heart's cry.

Psalm 56:8 says that God keeps records of our wanderings and places our tears in His bottle. Although at this point in my life I was not aware of this Scripture, I stand by its truth because of how God answered my prayer. A few days after my friend and I talked, she picked me up and took me to church with her. As I sat in this predominantly West Indian church, I noticed everyone was openly praying and crying to God. They were unashamed and free. It was both weird and remarkable to me.

In the church my family and I attended people never cried. Tears were saved for funerals. And the congregation never talked to God out loud. They simply repeated what the priest told them to say. Scripture, though, is filled with instances where people cried out, worshiped publicly and made joyful noises unto God. I was filled with holy envy watching others talk freely to my God. It was His way of helping me shift from outward religion to true worship.

I was witnessing Luke 12:8 in action. "And I tell you, everyone who acknowledges me before men, the Son of Man also will acknowledge before the angels of God." The people at this church were not afraid to talk to God in public. After I got over the initial shock, I was able to see freedom in their eyes. I wanted that badly. Up until that point I had only been that open with God in bed late at night or while I was in the shower, where no one could hear or see me.

The pastor called me up to the altar where others were already standing. I walked up nervously, and as he prayed for everyone who was standing there, I told God I needed an answer from heaven. My desire was to run away and leave everyone behind. The pastor walked over and laid his hand on my shoulder. He did not say anything out loud, but he must have been asking God to minister to me because after he walked away, I was overcome with an overwhelming emotion that I had never before experienced. My heart felt as if it was going to burst, and I began to sob uncontrollably. I dropped to my knees and wept. At that moment I knew God had taken over my life and was healing years of pain that I had stored deep inside.

When I felt like myself again, I got up and walked back to my seat. As I sat there assessing what had taken place, I remember vividly having a conversation with God. I told Him that I was grateful for His supernatural touch that had brought emotional healing to me. "The Spirit helps us in our weakness. For we do not know what to pray for as we ought, but the Spirit himself intercedes for us with groanings too deep for words" (Romans 8:26). That was exactly what was happening to me. I knew it was God, because this experience was completely different from all of the spiritual encounters that I had experienced with my family's Santería rituals. God's presence was holy and pure, and it felt like tangible love all over me. I had never known that God could be felt.

Up until that point I had thought that God was far away. I imagined Him up in heaven while we were on earth trying to get His attention with our petitions. I could not have been more wrong! God sent His Holy Spirit so that we could experience the Spirit of Christ living in us. The Holy Spirit is a person and is to be known personally. Unless we endeavor to have that moment by moment relationship with Jesus, we will be cutting ourselves off from being able to experience all of Him.

That day in church I did not expect to feel God, but I did expect to hear from God. He wrestled through all the cares of my life to touch my heart in a far greater way than I could have ever expected. That night I gave my heart to Jesus and asked Him what I was to do with my life. My career was going full speed, but so was my inner turmoil and the chaos in my environment at home.

I heard God respond to me, *Go back home and tell your mother and brother what you experienced.* Some of the church congregants drove me back home and waited in the car with me for hours as I continued to weep. God was doing surgery in my heart. He began removing hurt, pain, depression, suicidal thoughts, disappointment and abandonment. Meeting Jesus that day changed the trajectory of my life, and it opened me up to a world I knew nothing about.

Helmet of Salvation

There is an expression that declares that the two most important days of your life are the day you were born and the day you realize why you were born. When I experienced my friend's church service, I began to see the reason I was born.

I also received my first piece of spiritual armor. The Bible calls this piece of armor the helmet of salvation (see Ephesians 6:17). A helmet is a vital part of armor when you are going into battle. If your head is unprotected, the enemy has a clear shot by which he can take you out. The enemy also knows that if you go into a battle without your helmet of salvation, he is able to control your thoughts and emotions easily. With access to your mind, he can engage in psychological warfare and gain the advantage over you.

I made a trade with God that day in the storefront church. I laid down my sorrows, and He breathed new life into me. The enemy would not let me go without a fight, of course, but I now had my helmet of salvation to protect my mind from his lies. This protection allowed God to fully contend for me.

I obeyed God and went home and shared my experience with my mom and younger brother. I even asked my brother if he wanted me to pray that he would receive a touch from God. He did, and the next thing I knew, he fell down on the floor as if a wave of God's presence had washed over him and wrapped him in a blanket of love. Some Christians would call that being slain in the Spirit, but for us, we only knew that we were overcome by God's presence. I associate this act of reverence with the many times in the Bible that people encountered Jesus and fell to the ground or passed out (see Matthew 17:6; John 18:6; Revelation 1:17). This was something my brother had never witnessed before, but he was so open to God that He met him right there in the living room. The devil wanted me to run away, but God would not have it. He wanted me to go home, because He wanted to reveal Himself to my family, too.

Have you accepted Jesus into your heart and allowed Him to be your Savior, the Lord of your life? Have you traded your troubles for His joy and peace in your life? The Bible says this miraculous act of salvation is actually pretty simple; however, if you are not willing to surrender your will to Him, then the miracle will have no effect and nothing will change. "If you confess with your mouth that Jesus is Lord and believe in your heart that God raised him from the dead, you will be saved" (Romans 10:9).

This process is a beautiful exchange in which you shift the focus off of yourself and submit yourself to your Creator and His thoughts, plans and dreams for your life. In return, you gain freedom from the grip of sin, the enemy's lies and death. If you are a Christian you might know the following story, but in case you do not, I would like to share how deep the love of God goes in order to wrestle with anything that stands in the way of our souls.

In the Old Testament of the Bible, the prophet Isaiah shares God's promise to one day send a Savior in the form of a human to defeat evil and death and to create a new oath to heaven (see Isaiah 7:14). In the New Testament Paul also gives greetings to the people in the name of the Lord Jesus Christ, "who gave himself for our sins to deliver us from the present evil age, according to the will of our God and Father, to whom be glory forever and ever" (Galatians 1:4–5). In Leviticus we see that God instructed His people to shed the blood of spotless animals to make atonement for their transgressions (see 17:11). And Isaiah talks about the coming Messiah who would one day shed His own blood on the cross to defeat the hold that evil has on humanity.

But he was pierced for our transgressions; he was crushed for our iniquities; upon him was the chastisement that brought us peace, and with his wounds we are healed. All we like sheep have gone astray; we have turned—every one—to his own way; and the LORD has laid on him the iniquity of us all.

Isaiah 53:5–6

Likewise, Isaiah 61:1 says that the Messiah would come and proclaim the good news, bind up the brokenhearted, bring freedom for the captives and set mankind free from darkness. Jesus fulfilled this prophecy. The apostle John, who was a follower of Jesus, wrote, "For God so loved the world, that he gave his only Son, that whoever believes in him should not perish but have eternal life" (John 3:16).

Christ was born of a virgin as was foretold in Isaiah 7:14. He fulfilled the prophecies of old and lived a sinless life. He even told His followers, "This is my blood of the covenant, which is poured out for many for the forgiveness of sins" (Matthew 26:28). Because of Christ's death and His blood that was shed, God and humanity were restored. He was fully man but also fully God wrapped in flesh while He was on earth. "For if while we were enemies we were reconciled to God by the death of his Son, much more, now that we are reconciled, shall we be saved by his life" (Romans 5:10).

The enemy lost his grip on us through the shed blood of Jesus. His death was victory over the powers of darkness that try to enslave us with their deceitful ways. "He saved us, not because of works done by us in righteousness, but according to his own mercy, by the washing of regeneration and renewal of the Holy Spirit" (Titus 3:5).

When I gave my life to Christ, I somehow understood all of this as truth. I embraced eternal life and was willing to be transformed. I gave all authority in my life to Jesus—or at least that is what I thought. One of the root word translations of *salvation* in Hebrew is "deliverance." That was a continual process for me, and it would be a good five years before that happened fully.

The Word Is Our Weapon

I continued life as normal, because I really had no idea what having a relationship with God would look like. For years I had done things my own way. Once I gave my life to Jesus, He allowed me to take the time I needed to find my way to Him. The Word of God, however, came alive to me immediately and began to illuminate my path. I know that this was a supernatural intervention, because I had never much liked reading before, let alone reading the Bible.

Before I gave my life to Jesus, the enemy had a cloak over my eyes. Every time I picked up a Bible to read I became sleepy. I did not know it at the time, but it was spiritual oppression over me so that I would not desire God's Word to learn the truth of His love and freedom. I needed deliverance.

I have heard that many other people have had the same experience. Reading the King James Version probably was not the best idea for me at the time, either. My first language was a bunch of colloquialisms, and my second language was Spanglish. Needless to say, that version was extremely difficult for me to understand. "Your word is a lamp to my feet and a light to my path" (Psalm 119:105). That verse came alive to me once my eyes were opened to the truth.

At the same time, I was introduced to the new age teaching of *The Secret*, which is a book that takes biblical principles and mixes them with a range of spiritual beliefs and practices that are not scriptural. It is an imitation of godliness that lacks true power. The enemy of my soul hoped I would turn to that teaching and desert my newfound faith, but he was too late. The love of God had made a permanent impression on me, and I wanted more of His presence.

I used things such as positive thinking and the teachings of Word of Faith televangelists to help change my negative state of mind initially. I really needed to break free from a lifetime of negative thinking, and I wanted to know more about this Jesus who had captivated my heart. I used His incredible love letter to the world, the Holy Bible, to learn about Him. Paul tells us that "Scripture is breathed out by God and profitable for teaching, for reproof, for correction, and for training in righteousness" (2 Timothy 3:16). I was enrolled in the school of my God, but I still had a lot to learn.

While I was used to fighting in the natural world, I had no idea that the Bible instructs Christ-followers to use the Word of God as our sword. Our Bibles are part of our spiritual armor. Life has its fair share of conflict, but God fights our battles and gives us all the tools of protection that we need. The Word of God even fights our internal battles against the lies of the devil. "For the word of God is living and active, sharper than any two-edged sword, piercing to the division of soul and of spirit, of joints and of marrow, and discerning the thoughts and intentions of the heart" (Hebrews 4:12).

I had been so used to fighting with my words and my fists that I really had to study the Bible. I learned that when God said Jesus was our Savior, He meant it. Did you know that your words have the power to shape your world? Proverbs 18:21 says, "Death and life are in the power of the tongue." The Bible is clear that we will eat the fruits planted by the words we speak. "Let no corrupting talk come out of your mouths, but only such as is good for building up, as fits the occasion, that it may give grace to those who hear" (Ephesians 4:29). After many years of vulgarity and careless speech, I started to implement these truths in my life; however, the process was like trying to make a U-turn in a massive ship named Pessimistic Cruise Lines.

Your Heart Is Deceitfully Wicked

The devil was doing everything he could to destroy my life. Although I now had the tools I needed to win the battle against him, I still lacked wisdom. It would be a while before I would walk in my true fullness with God. I was hooked on wanting to know more about Jesus, and I absolutely loved the fact that I could reverse the years of negativity in my life by allowing God to renew my mind with His Word. But I still had one downfall, and that was misplaced loyalty.

I am a very loyal person. I think it is a combination of my father's family-first teachings and growing up in the hood. I had to learn that not everyone and everything should have my loyalty. As I continued to read the Bible, I started to learn what God considers right and wrong. I shared this with all of my loved ones, but I had soul ties with them all. A soul tie is a spiritual entanglement between two people that must be severed as they establish connections with God. Those ties kept me from going deeper with Him.

My "no man gets left behind" attitude caused me to give place to the wrong things. I thought I could win over my friends and my boyfriend by compromising with them. If I gave them what they wanted, then they would give me what I wanted, which was joining me at church.

This cycle left me in a world of hurt and disappointment. I believed that if they could feel what I felt from God, they would want to live for Him, too. If I could show them God's love, then they would understand and desire to do what was good; instead, the people in my life would appease me for a moment and then go right back to their ways. One of the church deacons once told me, "Whoever walks with the wise becomes wise, but the companion of fools will suffer harm" (Proverbs 13:20). I rejected what she said, though, because I could not abandon my friends and family. I was sure that they all needed me. I thought I needed to rescue them from themselves. What I did not know was that the devil was using my heart to deceive me.

I could never get a complete breakthrough, because I had emotional ties to this world. I had not surrendered my loved ones to God, and my attempts at carrying them drained my energy. Have you ever tried to convince yourself that your presence in people's lives is what is keeping them from getting worse? Have you felt you had to be loyal to people who were not loyal to God? My heart deceived me for many years, and it left me feeling exhausted. I was carrying baggage that God wanted me to put down.

It all came to a head while I was visiting Puerto Rico. It was my first time on my native island, and I was living my best life. As I went swimming at midnight in the bioluminescent water in Vieques, I looked up at heaven and was able to see a sky that was filled with stars. I looked down in the water and the microorganisms were glistening all over my body. I could not help but start praising God.

I was having the most glorious moment of my life—until I felt a burning sensation on my leg. I was being stung repeatedly by a jellyfish. I walked out of that experience with six severe welts on my body. While I was able to heal fully, I recognized that what had been below the surface of the water had wounded me and had ruined a beautiful time with the Father. God used that experience to show me that in the same way that the jellyfish sting had ruined a special moment with Him, I had been allowing others to pull me down and ruin my new relationship with God.

After I returned home, I knew things really had to change. How would I tell my loved ones that I needed to separate myself from their toxic lifestyles? How would I tell my boyfriend I could no longer engage in premarital sex? My heart fought me every inch of the way, but God's Spirit called me deeper. I knew that I was not supposed to act, speak or live how I had previously. I had invited God into my life, which was a start, but He wanted my heart. God was wrestling for my attention and my affection, and He did not want me to waste away helping those who would never listen.

This situation reminds me of a verse in Ephesians. "Let no unwholesome talk come out of your mouths, but only what is helpful for building up ones in need and bringing grace to those who listen. And do not grieve the Holy Spirit of God, in whom you were sealed for the day of redemption" (4:28–29 BSB). I had allowed loyalty to my loved ones to get in the way of my surrender to God, which grieved Him.

God went as far as taking away my hearing to help me understand that He was calling me to lay down those who stood in the way of my fulfilling His perfect will for my life. I came home from Puerto Rico with the intention of telling my boyfriend that we could no longer be intimate. We had a conversation in which I was firm, but he began to woo me and would not listen to what I was saying. He was persistent, and I stopped resisting eventually. Once it was over, I cried and asked him to leave.

The next morning, I woke up and I could not hear a thing. It was as if a bomb had gone off in my apartment causing everything to sound fuzzy and very far away. I was frightened and began to panic. I am a singer. I need to be able to hear. I began praying immediately and doing the spiritual practices I had seen in church. I grabbed a vial of anointing oil and prayed. As I pleaded, I heard in my spirit, *You would not listen, so I took away your hearing.* I became very frightened and cried desperately for God to forgive me. My hearing was restored a few days later, and through the process I learned that God will stop at nothing to get my attention.

What Do I See?

1. What experiences have you had where the enemy tried to steer you in one direction but God intervened?
2. In what ways (relationships, thoughts or actions) have you not allowed God to be fully present in your life?
3. What biblical words can you speak to fight the enemy in your own life?

What Can I Learn?

- You are in a spiritual battle even before you are saved, but God is fighting and contending on your behalf.

- God wishes to have an intimate, tangible relationship with you.
- Salvation means deliverance. God delivers us from evil.
- You cannot allow your heart to lead you. You must allow the Holy Spirit to be your leader.
- The Word of God is a weapon against the attack of the enemy.
- God will use situations in life to get our attention and lead us to repentance and surrender.

Scriptures for Meditation

Joshua 23:10
It is the LORD your God who fights for you, just as he promised you.

John 6:44
No one can come to me unless the Father who sent me draws him.

Hebrews 4:12
For the word of God is living and active, sharper than any two-edged sword, piercing to the division of soul and of spirit, of joints and of marrow, and discerning the thoughts and intentions of the heart.

Ephesians 4:30
And do not grieve the Holy Spirit of God, by whom you were sealed for the day of redemption.

Prayer and Declaration

Father God, in the name of Jesus, I thank You so much for always contending for me. Thank You for Your protection even when I did not know about it. Lord, I invite You again into my heart and life. Reveal Yourself to me and help me to have a tangible relationship with You. Help me to be bold and share my faith with others without compromising. Help me to walk in Your ways and resist the enemy and his deceitful traps. Lord, I pray that You would give me Your heart for people and the wisdom to know who I should or should not spend my time and energy with. Help me not to be deceived by my own desires. Help me to use Your Word as the lamp unto my feet and the sword with which I fight my battles. In Jesus' name, Amen.

8

Journey of a Half-Naked Preacher

A fter God saves us, we need to yield to the Holy Spirit so that He can sanctify us and make us into the image of Christ. At one point in our walk with God we have all been the "half-naked preacher." This phrase was something I began using to describe the very beginning of my Christian journey. It represents the period in my walk with the Lord when I was still in my flesh but was beginning to share Christ with others.

In order to graduate from that place of innocence, we need to be open to growing from glory to glory and avoiding staying stuck in our spiritual infancy. God has better for us. His love and His daily presence make us holy. In this chapter, I will help you discover the roadblocks that might be standing in your way, and I will help you find and stay on the path to living a holy life.

Mixing God and the World

God loved me, and now I knew it. I could feel Him stronger than any inclination of evil I had ever felt growing up in witchcraft. This was a game changer for me. Not only was a relationship with God palpable, His love was unconditional. Although my life was a noticeable wreck, I felt no judgment from Him. I was at the height of my pop career, and the Creator had solidified my purpose.

I continued to attend the small church where these strange people shouted unashamedly to God. When I was not in church, I was out doing my job, singing to sold-out crowds who adored my bad girl, tell-it-like-it-is persona. My heart had begun to change, but it would be a long time before everything else caught up.

"Put God first!" I shouted to fans after every concert. I was half dressed and had gyrated up and down the stage for forty minutes. I probably even dropped a few f-bombs in between songs while sharing about my crazy life, but I did not want to leave these impressionable people without letting them know that the only reason a girl from the hood was on that stage with thousands singing her lyrics was because God was real and had given her a purpose. Sure, I credited my success to all my hard work, and I wanted the crowd to desire me, but I also wanted them to know God was real and that they were never alone. My spiritual heart had begun to change, but the pride of life still had a grip on me. I needed to be purified.

Every time I spoke about God during a concert, the blanket of drunken, lustful, self-indulgence that was over the crowd lifted enough for me to see the longing in their eyes. I had won over their trust, so I had their undivided attention and could speak into their lives. I still remember how each time I mentioned God people would well up with emotion. It was as if they looked at me with their souls crying out, "Please do not leave me here." I did not understand, however, that the power of influence and the platform I stood on gave me a door to reach them. I gave everyone a bread crumb of hope and assumed it was enough. We all can find ourselves open to hearing something about God because He tugs on our hearts. Unfortunately, I did not know enough to give anyone the tools they needed to go beyond that point.

Backstage, I was strict in my routine: no drinking, no drugs (around me) and no performance without prayer. It felt like the right thing to do. Although my mini skirt, crop top, ego and vulgar mouth were not at all honoring to God, the fact that I had invited Him in with prayer always created a spiritual shield around me. Have you had moments in your life where you knew God would not be pleased with where you were, but you knew He was with you anyway? Yeah, that was me. I always excused it because I thought, *Hey, I am at work.*

When I was not on a stage, I was in the recording studio. I heard a preacher say that we should share God with everyone, so I made that my goal. At this point in my career, I had gained enough traction to work with some of the industry's best. My collaborators consisted of world-renowned pop producers who represented many different expressions of faith, including atheists and Muslims. I tried to share with each of them my newfound passion that it was possible to know and experience God. How could I not share this incredible experience with the world? I wanted everyone to know that fame and status do not compare to having an encounter with God.

Working in a studio for seven hours a day is a bonding experience, and I hoped that I was getting through to them with my Christian message. Little did I know that they were allowing me to burn their ears off with my experiences because it was wasting time that my record label was paying for. While I am not sure if my efforts in sharing the truth helped them, none of them can say they did not hear about God's love.

Paul says, "With eager hope, the creation looks forward to the day when it will join God's children in glorious freedom from death and decay. For we know that all creation has been groaning as in the pains of childbirth right up to the present time" (Romans 8:20–22 NLT). I believe every person I come in contact with who does not have the knowledge of the hope of Jesus is likewise crying out. They should know what Jesus did for them.

Jesus tells a story about Lazarus—who was a destitute man with sores all over his body—and a rich man (see Luke 16). Jesus explained to His disciples that while Lazarus was alive, he begged the rich man to share with him, even if it was the crumbs from his table. But the rich man shunned him every time. They both died suddenly, and Lazarus went to be with Abraham (the father of his Jewish faith) in a place of comfort and peace. The rich man, however, went to Hades, a place of great torment. Jesus explained that the rich man saw Lazarus from Hades and begged Lazarus to give him a drop of water because he was in anguish due to the flames surrounding him. After realizing there was no hope or consolation, the rich man pleaded with Abraham to send Lazarus back from the dead to warn his family of their impending doom so that they could have a different fate. Abraham responded, "If they won't listen to Moses and the prophets, they won't be persuaded even if someone rises from the dead" (Luke 16:31 NLT).

This story stirred me to share my faith with others. How sad is it that people in hell will suffer such torment? Every chance I get I want to share about the redemption of Jesus; however, I believe that the best way to minister to someone is for them to see your faith lived out.

Half-Naked Preacher

When I was not in the studio or on tour, I was at church learning everything I could about this God who was sweeping me off my feet. Since I had no concept of church culture, I wore the same clothes that I wore to the studio or the club to church, which was normally tight jeans and a crop top that showed off my belly button. I genuinely did not have any other options and truly thought nothing of it. I had no knowledge of what spiritual conviction was.

I later learned that conviction is a feeling that you get that says, *You probably shouldn't do that.* If you are like me, after ignoring that voice several times and thinking that you know best, you realize that it is God's way of gently helping you not to ruin your life. I still pray for God to convict me of the things I may not be aware of that are not pleasing to Him.

Sadly, although I did not know it at the time, the people at the church I was a part of were judging me and staying clear of me until I cleaned up my act. The pastor and his wife would pray for me at church, but that was the extent of that relationship. The church deacons had a different approach.

These leaders who I barely knew told me that I was still a street girl and that I should quit singing secular music and wearing tight clothes. For me, their comments were more fuel in the hater's tank. They made me want to be even more rebellious. I still remember my response to one of the deacons who told me bluntly that my pants would cause the men in the church to stumble.

I said, "Even if I had a garbage bag on, men would still look." Yikes! Although the statement might have been true, I really had no idea how to protect myself from temptation, let alone care about helping someone else who was struggling with lust.

Here is where the disconnect was for me. God loved me and I felt Him near. He was loving on me before He began changing the things He wanted to change. But no one took the time to have a relationship with me or mentor me on my walk. Because no one in the church had gained my trust, I felt the same things I had always felt from people growing up: envy, judgment and ill wishes. It felt as if they were betting on my downfall rather than hoping I would succeed in my new faith walk.

I did not have a clue as to why I should dress differently. I had no idea that my filthy mouth was not honoring to God. I did not know that attaining success for myself was not God's best for me—especially when the country I was raised in, America, promoted all of those things as good things. I did not know that God's ways are different from our ways. All I knew is that God loved me so much that He was reaching out to me in tangible ways.

Look at your own life. Would you say God and the truth in the Bible influence you most, or is your life a reflection of the worldly culture and the things your non-Christian loved ones have taught you? At that time, I fitted into the latter part of that question.

I want to make something very clear about this sanctification process. It is something between you and God, and it is developed as you grow in Him. If your life is not evolving to become more like Jesus, then chances are you are not growing in your spiritual walk. In this Christian life, we are either growing or dying—there is no in between. Neutrality is a trick of the enemy. It is a pathway to nominalism and being lukewarm. The Bible is clear about how Jesus feels concerning lukewarm believers. It says that they are spat out (see Revelation 3:16).

Because I still felt God's presence and He continued speaking to me, I thought that meant I had arrived and nothing about me had to be changed. I would go to church and feel the Holy Spirit—I would cry or fall to my knees, I would have a supernatural experience, I would close my eyes and see visions from God, or I would hear God give me specific instructions about key areas in my life—but that did not mean I was inviting the Holy Spirit to really take residence in me full time. I reserved God moments for church. I was so naïve that I thought church was the only place that I was supposed to experience Him.

I was committed to going to church every chance I could to learn more about this amazing God who was letting me experience Him more than I ever thought I could. The issue was, however, that as soon as I left the church, I went back to acting how I always had. The heavens were shut, and I could only access God in minute-long prayers late at night when the rest of the world was sleeping, or when I was in the shower. For me, there is something about a shower that sets the stage to have the best one-on-one times with God.

Remember, I had no example of what church people acted like outside of a church service. Because of this, I kept doing what I always had done. As the first born-again Christian in my immediate family, I would love on God in church and then love on the world when I was not in church. That meant acting how the world expected me to act: foulmouthed, seductive and prideful. The only thing that really changed was that I was sure to insert God into the conversation here and there. I had a new love in my life. He had begun to captivate my heart, so I could not help but bring Him into my world. It is true that "out of the abundance of the heart the mouth speaks" (Matthew 12:34 NKJV). I could not help but speak about Jesus; however, because I was still worldly, I also continued using unwholesome talk.

Heavenly War Within

After four years of following this routine with no real mentor or spiritual guidance, other than my flesh and what I could learn at church services, I started to feel as if there was a spiritual battle waging within me. I broke off my relationship with my boyfriend-turned-fiancé. I realized that he was not in a place to follow me on my journey with God. And probably because I wasted so much of their studio money preaching, my record label parted ways with me. The bad girl they once signed had become a half-naked preacher who could not stop talking about Jesus.

I also invited the witches in my family to church. That is when I began to see spiritual contention play out before my eyes. Like a scene from a wild west movie, a duel between good and evil, the pastor and the high priestess in my family were in an all-out silent war in the heavenlies. At the end of the day, the pastor always had home-court advantage. Through this my eyes were opened to light and darkness. Unfortunately, the people in my family opposed God because they had made a pact with their religion.

One night at a prayer service I felt a wrestling match begin inside of me. I could feel something moving within my belly as the pastor spoke of spiritual oppression. When he asked if anyone felt as if they were battling a demonic force, I slipped up my hand without even thinking. I found myself at the altar rededicating my life to Jesus. Everyone in the church began to pray for me to be free from demonic influence. I coughed, I gagged, and I even spat as I was told to release whatever was in me. Although I felt some relief, I knew that the battle was not over. At the end of the service I told the pastor that I still felt things inside me battling it out. That prompted a few of the church leaders to come back to my apartment to help me get rid of items that they believed were open doors to the enemy.

This would be the first time I realized that our possessions have the ability to host things in the spiritual realm. All the things the church leaders pointed out in my house were gifts from family members who had been steeped in witchcraft, including the crown that I was given on my Sweet 16. The church leaders had no idea where I had gotten any of those items, but as they walked through my house like Holy Ghost detectives who asked God to reveal to them items that were not of God, they kept pointing things out that were given to me by those particular family members.

Clean Yourself and Your Space

Have you ever looked through your home with your spiritual eyes? I had never done that, nor did I think I had to. From that point on, however, I lived by the phrase "When in doubt, throw it out." If something I own or have been given makes me question the item or the source of the item, I let it go. This also applies to the things that I shop for. Souvenirs or handmade jewelry can be items that have been committed to other gods. We bring them into our homes because we think they make us look cultured, but honestly, it is not worth it!

Not only did I need a spiritual cleaning, but my home needed a physical cleaning. We do not often realize that the gifts we bring into our homes can bring a curse upon us. After that day, it was clear to me that Old Testament Scriptures concerning what you bring into your house still apply today. "Do not bring any detestable objects into your home, for then you will be destroyed, just like them. You must utterly detest such things, for they are set apart for destruction" (Deuteronomy 7:26 NLT). God even instructed the Old Testament priests to anoint with oil every piece of furniture brought into the tabernacle "so that it may become holy" (Exodus 40:9).

After the church leaders helped me get rid of the demonic access points in my home, we prayed collectively for God's presence to invade my home and everything in it. I look at it this way: If possessions can be holy, then that means they can also be unholy. At this point in my life, I had experienced enough oppression. I did not want to settle for being open-minded—I wanted God, and God is holy. When the church leaders left my home very late that night, I felt a weight lift, and the wrestling in my stomach ceased. For the first time in my life I renounced every tie to spiritual darkness, from my upbringing to my own actions. I began to change quickly.

My immediate family was falling apart, my friends were missing in action, my fiancé whom I had lived with for two years was now gone, and the dream I had worked hard to have was up in the air. I should have been devastated, but I felt liberated, instead. I was free to explore this new love I had. I had thousands of adoring fans, and yet all I wanted was an audience of one. To Him, I was not half naked. He knew all of me, flaws and all, and He wanted to give me a better life than I had experienced previously. Now that all the clutter was gone, I felt less distraction and more curiosity about all the things of God I still had to learn. Jesus had my attention. The red carpet had been pulled out from under me, and all I could do was look up.

I was 21 years old, clinging to the only consistent thing I had ever had—God. That is when I asked Him the most important question of my life. "Do you have a plan for me?"

Sanctification—RIP Me

Not only were my spiritual eyes opened, but now my ears were, too. All along Jesus had created a plan for my life, but I could not see it until He removed all of my idols. As a loyal person I wanted to dedicate to God the same amount of faithfulness that He had shown to me. I recognized that He had always been faithful even when I had not been. I invited His presence to come and saturate my house, and I prayed actively that He would ban evil spirits from my dwelling. Those actions turned my home into a sanctuary. I still anoint my home with oil as a sign of consecrating my home to Him. I use the oil as a point of contact and as a symbol of the Holy Spirit. At times, I also prayed with a prayer shawl from Israel that my pastor gave me.

Now that my distractions had been removed and I had ample time on my hands, I dove headfirst into everything that centered around God. I could see my need for holiness and purity, and I wanted to be a good reflection of this real and faithful God. I flung open my Bible, and I asked the Holy Spirit to deliver me from cursing, perversion, anger and unforgiveness. I needed God's best for me to replace the years of dysfunction.

I started to experience a supernatural hunger for righteousness. Lo and behold, I was delivered from the things that had been ingrained in me for many years. That hunger for righteousness caused me to begin doing righteous things. I was not bewitched by a church or religion to do what was right. I wanted to do what was right genuinely because of God's great love that engulfed me.

This spiritual awakening caused what God had already planted inside of me to have an expression and actions. I now wanted to show mercy because mercy was shown to me. I had compassion for those who had hurt me the most. God replaced my worldly coated glasses with His eyes of forgiveness and grace. I often describe Luke 7:47 as my life verse: "Therefore, I tell you, her many sins have been forgiven—as her great love has shown. But whoever has been forgiven little loves little" (NIV). I was that sinful woman who was now forgiven, and I could not help but want to extend the same mercy to those around me. I did not deserve one ounce of forgiveness, but He still welcomed me to Him with open arms.

During this time, I found my secret place with Jesus. I took time to seek Him, and each time that I did I listened for His direction and asked for an experience in His presence. I was desperate for Him. I would not move until He moved. Every time God revealed something to me, I knew it was because He wanted to heal me. Because of this, I learned true surrender. Eventually, I no longer looked as I had looked, and no strong language came out of my mouth. God's love turned me into a lady who wanted to dress like a princess for her king. I even allowed Him to melt my heart of unforgiveness toward my family.

We all have moments in life where we can choose to go down the path of purity and righteousness. This path helps us begin the process of getting cleaned up. We all fall into sin, but as my favorite band, Switchfoot, sings, I believe our "native tongue" is love. Learning how much God loves us and embracing Him causes us to walk in His ways.

Have you had moments in your life when you could have chosen to do what was right, but that path seemed like the harder path to choose because you wanted to do the opposite? God does not leave you to figure it out on your own. When Jesus left this earth, He sent us His Holy Spirit to help us walk in God's ways and to become new women and men who are able to put on holiness and righteousness. His Spirit helps us to be incredible reflections of this incredible God.

What Do I See?

1. What old habits or mindsets may be a hindrance to God abiding in your life?
2. What possessions do you have that might be blocking your spiritual health?

3. How is God working in your life right now to make you more like Jesus?

What Can I Learn?

- God loves us even when we are unlovely.
- What is in your heart will come out of your mouth. If Jesus is in your heart, you will find yourself talking about Him.
- Sanctification is a process. Be patient with yourself and trust the work of the Holy Spirit in your life.
- Possessions can host spirits. Do a spiritual check of your life and home for things that might be holding you back.
- If we expect to grow, we have to be open to change and willing to bring all our brokenness, unholiness and burdens to Him. Change can be hard, but godly change brings about God's best for us.
- God's presence in you is what makes you holy. More time with Him means more of His presence, which means more growth in righteousness.

Scriptures for Meditation

1 Samuel 10:6

"Then the Spirit of the LORD will rush upon you, and you will prophesy with them and be turned into another man [or woman]."

2 Peter 1:4–7 NKJV

Be partakers of the divine nature, having escaped the corruption that is in the world through lust. But also for this very reason, giving all diligence, add to your faith virtue, to virtue knowledge, to knowledge self-control, to self-control perseverance, to perseverance godliness, to godliness brotherly kindness, and to brotherly kindness love.

2 Timothy 2:21

Therefore, if anyone cleanses himself from what is dishonorable, he will be a vessel for honorable use, set apart as holy, useful to the master of the house, ready for every good work.

1 Thessalonians 5:23

Now may the God of peace himself sanctify you completely, and may your whole spirit and soul and body be kept blameless at the coming of our Lord Jesus Christ.

Prayer and Declaration

Father, in the name of Jesus, I come to You today asking for the power of Your Holy Spirit to engulf me. Wash me clean of anything that is not of You. Deliver me from all evil, known and unknown, and from the sins of my past. Give me spiritual eyes to discern the things in my life and home that need to be changed or tossed out. Wash me as white as snow. Give me a greater desire for You and Your righteousness. Reveal Your purpose for my life. Forgive me for trying to satisfy my longings with anything other than You. You are my only true hope, my refuge and the lover of my soul. I commit my life, my actions and my deeds to You. Cause me to walk in Your ways and to be a vessel for honorable use, set apart as holy, useful and ready for every good work. Thank You that my entire spirit, soul and body will be kept blameless. I declare this in the name above every name. In Jesus' name, Amen.

9

Deliverance Is Found in God's Presence

The more you delve into getting to know God the greater your perspective on yourself, on Him, on life and on others becomes. God, the creator of everything, the one who holds the galaxies in His hands, knows you by name and hand-picked you to be His. He wants to have a one-on-one relationship with you. Many people understand this truth only with head knowledge, but it can go further than that. He grants us the ability to know Him experientially. In this chapter, we will dive into some of the ways we can press into God's presence and truly have the intimate relationship many of His followers, such as David and Paul, talked about in the Bible. The relationships they achieved caused them to shift the culture of their day.

The Only One Who Satisfies

Before really surrendering to God, I only cried out to Him to satisfy my wants and needs. I never even thought to ask Him what His will was for my life. All of these great things happened to me: I made it out of the hood, I became successful, I averted teen pregnancy and I avoided getting involved in drugs or drinking. Still, I always prayed for God to give me more. He sent manna from heaven to help me make it out of the bondage I was in, but that was not good enough for me. I wanted what I wanted. It was not until my life changed and I began my true relationship with God at the helm that I became extremely aware that everything else I had in life kept me wanting more.

Those successes could not satisfy. Jesus is the only one who truly satisfies. He declared, "I am the bread of life; whoever comes to me shall not hunger, and whoever believes in me shall never thirst" (John 6:35). Your time with Him is what determines the results of your entire life. Spending time in His presence is where you get vitality, proper perspective, authority and power to do the miraculous.

I truly believe time in the presence of God is the answer to everything in life. Morality and Christianity are not the same. There are really good people who are kind, healthy, smart and even serene, but they do not have the power to shift an atmosphere or the ability to heal the sick. They cannot help others out of demon possession or lead themselves to eternal hope.

Dancing on the Moon

I was now a young adult and lived in my own apartment. I had nothing but time. The distractions were removed, so I could finally focus on creating a real relationship with God. He desires to have fellowship with His creation. In fact, that relationship is why we were created. But the enemy has made it his goal to interfere with this fellowship.

God knows how to get our attention. As I write this book the world is experiencing a global pandemic. Because of this, everyone is forced to stay at home and distance themselves from others. They cannot go to their jobs or participate in extracurricular activities. Monumental experiences such as these throughout biblical history have been moments when God's people either held on tightly to Him or perished. In my experience, the more I delve into God the greater my relationship with Him becomes. I started to invite God into every part of my life.

"Good morning, Lord. I am so happy to have another day of life with you by my side. Would you sit with me and have breakfast?"

"What do you think I should wear?"

"Would you meet with me a while?"

I wanted the presence of God to be a part of every moment of my life. "Do you not know that your body is a temple of the Holy Spirit within you, whom you have from God? You are not your own" (1 Corinthians 6:19). Jesus also told His followers that the Holy Spirit would live with those who called on the name of the Lord (see John 14). With those passages in mind, I made sure to acknowledge God moment by moment.

Along with reading the Bible, praying and talking with God, I was determined to have supernatural experiences every time I was in His presence. I wanted all of God and was hungry to experience all that He freely gives access to. Jesus said, "Blessed are those who hunger and thirst for righteousness, for they shall be satisfied" (Matthew 5:6). I wanted to dream supernatural dreams, to see visions and to audibly hear from God. Because of my desire to experience God in these ways and my dedication to spending time with Him in expectancy, I encountered God in tangible ways that revolutionized my life.

There were times I closed my eyes and asked God to meet me in the most beautiful parts of my imagination. In those moments, I fell deeper and deeper in love with Him. My secret place with Him would transport me from New York to the mountaintops in Israel, to a beach in Hawaii or even to dance with Him on the moon. I took the limits off of God, and He revealed Himself to me in limitless ways. This relationship gave me the spiritual fortitude to know that I did not have to fear anything the enemy tried to send my way. God's love drowned out all of the noise, and for the first time in my entire existence I allowed His love to permeate my world, my thoughts and my heart. His love began to rewrite my story, showing me my true identity in Him. "Whoever has my commands and keeps them is the one who loves me. The one who loves me will be loved by my Father, and I too will love them and show myself to them" (John 14:21 NIV).

Release a Sound

How do Christians differ from others? It is His presence that makes the difference. Many people have said, "But I go to church and I don't feel anything different. I tried praying, but nothing happens so I just give up." The Bible tells us, "Draw near to God, and he will draw near to you" (James 4:8). He does not ignore the sincere beckoning of His children. He has already provided everything we need by grace; however, we do have a job. It is to come in agreement with Him and release a sound of faith. When we do, we position ourselves to receive what was already given to us by God.

The sound of our prayers, conversations with God and our worship of Him grants us access to the divine spiritual realm that was already given to us when Jesus reconciled us to God. As a worship leader, I understand the implications of lifting up a sound of sincere praise to God. I have seen the power of worship shift the atmosphere. I have seen the presence of God come in as a flood and break through the natural threshold into the spiritual realm, thus inviting heaven to come down.

In Genesis, we read that God said, "Let there be light" (1:3). I believe the author shared with us the importance and the power of releasing a sound into the earth's atmosphere. In the natural, sound moves through vibrations. When God said, "Let there be light," He showed us that a sound has the power to create. Through the story of Jericho and what happened to that city's walls, we see that a sound can also destroy.

> "On the seventh day you shall march around the city seven times, and the priests shall blow the trumpets. And when they make a long blast with the ram's horn, when you hear the sound of the trumpet, then all the people shall shout with a great shout, and the wall of the city will fall down flat."
>
> Joshua 6:4–5

New age folks and other religions break this down into frequencies, which is where they get their belief about karma.

As Christians, however, we know that we do not get what we truly deserve. If we did, we would all be condemned to hell. That is why we release a sound of thanksgiving and adoration to our God.

It is important to stay in the presence of God at all times so that we avoid the influence of the god of this world and his demonic rebel spirits. The phrase *Yahweh Sabaoth* is found all throughout the Old Testament (see Psalm 24:10). It describes God as the Lord of hosts, and its root word means "to wage war." By this description we see that God is the all-conquering Savior and the commander of the invisible armies. We, as God's children, need not be afraid or affected by the enemy, because He who is in us is greater.

Before His death, Jesus told Pontius Pilot that His Kingdom was not of this world (see John 18:36). He made it clear that there was a spiritual reality and that His Kingdom was a heavenly one. He wanted His followers to live a life that reflected His Kingdom instead of chasing the cares of this life. It is not easy to stay in His presence in a world that is filled with distraction.

Sometimes it seems as if everyone in my generation and younger has ADD, or Attention Deficit Disorder. We are all distracted easily. I believe it is A Demon of Distraction, which has the same acronym as Attention Deficit Disorder: ADD. I am sure there are medical conditions that heighten one's inability to stay focused, but that is not what I am referring to. I am talking about the struggle many people have to sit in prayer and draw near to God without grabbing their phones, thinking about something else they need to be doing or getting distracted by other things. After losing all of my idols, my career, all the people around me, etc., I was finally in a place to see everything clearly. Nothing else satisfies.

These one-on-one experiences with God had such a deep impact on me that I penned a couple of songs about them. See some of the lyrics below:

LOVED BY YOU

I can't believe it,
How I'm feeling so invincible.
I cannot see it,
How You love me unconditional.
I'm so committed.
What we have they can't beat it.
It's irreplaceable.
You came and conquered,
Liberated every part of me.
You won't forsake me.
You ain't leaving,
That's a guarantee.
You're my beginning.
You're with me,
Then I'm winning.
There's nothing I can't do.
I can dance across the moon with You.
I can sail across the deep blue.
I'm so happy to be alive.
So happy You're by my side.
So glad that I'm in love with You.
I can skate along the clouds with You,
And I'll never have to leave the room.
Up so high I'm holding tight.
My world here just comes alive.
It's all from being loved by You.

DANCING WITH JESUS

People stare and say I'm crazy,
'Cuz they don't understand what's happening, no.
Oh, this light's so bright it's blinding me.
But what's to see when you feel everything.
I knew this day was different, nothing like before.
Oh, so close in distance, He's got me wanting more.
And I feel His presence, and it's moving me.
How can I deny it—I never felt so free.
What am I feeling?
I'm crying and screaming but laughing, rejoicing.
I'm dancing with Jesus.

Power in His Presence

I am sure that you have heard of the saying, "You are what you eat." People say this phrase to help promote a healthy lifestyle. The same goes for your spiritual appetite. When you accept Christ into your heart, you invite His Spirit to come into your life. The presence of God is what makes us whole, healthy and strong. Jesus tells us what filling ourselves with Him looks like.

> "Abide in me, and I in you. As the branch cannot bear fruit by itself, unless it abides in the vine, neither can you, unless you abide in me. I am the vine; you are the branches. Whoever abides in me and I in him, he it is that bears much fruit, for apart from me you can do nothing. If anyone does not abide in me he is thrown away like a branch and withers; and the branches are gathered, thrown into the fire, and burned."
>
> John 15:4–6

After His death and resurrection, Jesus told His followers that He would make it easier for them to abide in Him and move in His power. He would send the Holy Spirit as their helper. "But you will receive power when the Holy Spirit has come upon you, and you will be my witnesses in Jerusalem and in all Judea and Samaria, and to the end of the earth" (Acts 1:8). Any successful Christian must stay connected to the vine, Jesus, and gain his or her nourishment from His Spirit.

When we are connected with God, we have access to all that He promises us. The more we get to know Him the more we learn what He knows. As I started to seek Him and discover what that really meant, I began to see myself in relation to Him. Oh, how wretched I am compared to such a holy and pure God! It is unfathomable to think that He would cover me in His righteousness and give me access to all that He has, even though I do not deserve it. And all I had to do was want to spend time in His presence.

As I stayed hidden in and connected to God, I learned about taking authority. I no longer had to allow the enemy to overtake me. I had capacity in the limitless God in whom I abided to fight off the enemy's attacks. I developed a godly confidence and understood what Jesus promised when He said, "I have given you authority to tread on serpents and scorpions, and over all the power of the enemy, and nothing shall hurt you" (Luke 10:19).

Suddenly, the phrases I often heard in church made sense. Two of those were "Covered by the blood of Jesus" and "No weapon that is fashioned against you shall succeed" (Isaiah 54:17). I was so far hidden under the shadow of the almighty God that evil could not come anywhere near me.

During this time, I often found myself out late recording music and coming home on a New York City subway that traveled through a crime-filled neighborhood. But I was not afraid of anything. God was all over me and He stood before me. I felt bulletproof. I had a hedge of protection all around me, because I always made it safely to and from where I was going.

When I think about the power that comes with spending time in the presence of God, I think about King David before he was even a king. He was only a shepherd boy, forgotten by his own family and spending time on his own looking after his family's pasture. During that time by himself, he drew near to God. David is said to have had a heart after God's own heart. When you read through his songs and poems in the book of Psalms you get a better sense of the beautiful intimacy he shared with God.

When he heard about Goliath's threat against the Jewish people, he thought nothing of handling that threat in the name of his God. Check out his response to King Saul about the giant.

> "Let no man's heart fail because of him [Goliath]. Your servant will go and fight with this Philistine." And Saul said to David, "You are not able to go against this Philistine to fight with him, for you are but a youth, and he has been a man of war from his youth." But David said to Saul, "Your servant used to keep sheep for his father. And when there came a lion, or a bear, and took a lamb from the flock, I went after him and struck him and delivered it out of his mouth. And if he arose against me, I caught him by his beard and struck him and killed him. Your servant has struck down both lions and bears, and this uncircumcised Philistine shall be like one of

them, for he has defied the armies of the living God." And David said, "The LORD who delivered me from the paw of the lion and from the paw of the bear will deliver me from the hand of this Philistine." And Saul said to David, "Go, and the LORD be with you!'"

1 Samuel 17:32–37

Goliath was nothing to young David, because David knew who his God was in relation to any threat. People who focus on other things more than God will be consumed by what they are focused on. It is important for us to stay connected to the source of life. We need to stay hidden in His presence so that we can approach the giants of life with the same godly courage that David did in his battle. The giants of depression, suicidal thoughts, addiction, financial crisis or any other demonic attack on our families cannot stand against our God.

David had spent the time needed in the presence of God to access the authority given freely to the sons and daughters of God. The attack of the enemy should be nothing if you realize that it is God's presence in you with which the enemy is contending. Jesus told us, "In the world you will have tribulation. But take heart; I have overcome the world" (John 16:33). Moses also understood this principle when he told God, "If your presence will not go with me, do not bring us up from here" (Exodus 33:15).

Paul said, "Through the church the manifold wisdom of God might now be made known to the rulers and authorities in the heavenly places" (Ephesians 3:10). It is not by our own strength that we have to battle. If we invite the Spirit of God to move freely through us, we will really see change.

My prayer for you is this: "May He grant you out of the riches of His glory, to be strengthened and spiritually energized with power through His Spirit in your inner self, [indwelling your innermost being and personality]" (Ephesians 3:16 AMP).

How Do You Access God's Power?

During my one-on-one time with God, I realized that reading God's Word gave me life, encouragement and great wisdom. It also led me to hunger for a deeper relationship with Him. It was then that I realized there was another level in which God wanted to connect with me beyond the confines of the spiritual chores I had begun doing. Even as I prayed, I would mouth off everything I was thinking, feeling and what I wanted God to do, but I rarely stopped to see what He was saying in return. Imagine if I had treated one of my loved ones that way? We must invite Him into our devotional time.

Picture this: You pick up your Bible and read it while God sits across from you trying to get your attention. You never once look up to invite Him into your time of reading. Or, imagine this scenario: You invite Jesus over to your house. When He arrives, you greet Him and start talking a million miles per minute, never once stopping to hear what He has to say in return.

Along with practicing spiritual disciplines, God wants us to invite Him into the time that we dedicate for Him. In that time of sitting with God, He deposits things into our spirits that can change our lives and the lives of everyone around us. When I started practicing this, I always had a notebook ready. He would start talking to my spirit and give me instructions for my life.

He gave me visions of the most elaborate things, and I gained supernatural strength and endurance. It was like a high that came from heaven. The time that I spent with God in His presence invigorated me, even if I had not slept much the night before or if I had been fasting. It healed me of whatever I was dealing with, and it gave me the strength to go out and do whatever it was He had instructed me to do. It was in times such as these that I learned how to navigate being saved by God in a world that despises His ways.

I often hear that people do not spend time with God because every time they try, they are either too busy or it is too late at night. But I heard a sermon preached recently that really convicted me. It was based on the first chapter of Mark, and it looked at how, even during really busy days, Jesus communicated consistently with the heavenly Father. If you read all of Mark 1, you will see what a typical day in Jesus' life looked like.

Jesus began His day by teaching at the synagogue. While there, He drove out an impure spirit. After that, He went to a disciple's house and ended up healing Simon Peter's mother-in-law, who was sick. As the day changed into night, people from all around town brought the sick to where He was. He then healed many and drove out demons from some who were possessed.

That is a lot, right? I am exhausted even thinking about it. If I had done all of that, I would probably tell my friends and family that I needed a week off to sleep and do nothing. The next verse, however, shows us the importance of spending time with God. Jesus knew where His power came from, and it was not from earthly rest, energy boosters or working out tirelessly. He knew His strength came from time with the heavenly Father.

Mark 1:35 reveals what He did after that power-packed day. "And rising very early in the morning, while it was still dark, he departed and went out to a desolate place, and there he prayed." I believe this verse is included to show us that our outward power (spiritual and physical) can be linked to our one-on-one time with God. "But when you pray, go into your room and shut the door and pray to your Father who is in secret. And your Father who sees in secret will reward you" (Matthew 6:6).

Never before had I thought I would be able to speak in new languages, cast demons out of people, or pray for healing until I spent that one-on-one time with God and became His student. Jesus instructed His followers that as they received healing, deliverance and heavenly blessings, they were to pay it forward to others. "Heal the sick, raise the dead, cure those with leprosy, and cast out demons. Give as freely as you have received" (Matthew 10:8 NLT).

As a follower of Jesus, that is my goal. It should be your goal, too. We will not be able to do any of these things unless we are accessing our power from the source of all power. God wants to have one-on-one time with us. In His presence, the powers of darkness cannot prevail, and we are granted the ability to do all the aforementioned and more.

What Do I See?

1. What does releasing your own sound of faith look like?
2. Which distractions that you struggle with take time away from having intimate moments in God's presence?

3. What are some ways you can improve your one-on-one time with God?

4. What are some areas of your life that you want to take authority over?

What Can I Learn?

- A sound of faith provides a way for you to access the power from on high that Jesus promised.
- We have the power to shift a negative atmosphere into a positive atmosphere when we release our sound of faith.
- God is looking more for one-on-one time with you than He is for your commitment to spiritual chores.
- Ask God to show you things in the supernatural realm.
- Time in the presence of God builds your spiritual confidence in Him and in who He created you to be.
- Power to slay the giants in your life only comes through your connection to God.
- You receive freely from God while spending time with Him. Freely share that with others.

Scriptures for Meditation

John 14:21 NIV
"Whoever has my commands and keeps them is the one who loves me. The one who loves me will be loved by my Father, and I too will love them and show myself to them."

Jeremiah 33:3

"Call to me and I will answer you, and will tell you great and hidden things that you have not known."

Matthew 5:6

"Blessed are those who hunger and thirst for righteousness, for they shall be satisfied."

Luke 10:19

"I have given you authority to tread on serpents and scorpions, and over all the power of the enemy, and nothing shall hurt you."

Exodus 33:15

"If your presence will not go with me, do not bring us up from here."

Ephesians 3:16 AMP

May He grant you out of the riches of His glory, to be strengthened and spiritually energized with power through His Spirit in your inner self [indwelling your innermost being and personality].

Prayer and Declaration

Father, in the name of Jesus I come to You with my whole heart and undivided attention. Lord, I long to meet with You and share a true intimate relationship with You. Have mercy on me for allowing the cares of this life to distract me. I set my affections on You, and I ask that You reveal Yourself to me in a deeper way.

May I get a true revelation of who You are and who I am in You. May I continue to hunger and thirst for time with You. I cannot wait to be in Your presence. Infuse me with power from on high to overcome evil and to walk in the authority You have given to me as your child. Every day I will draw near to You, seek You and find You. Thank You for Your presence. In Jesus' name, Amen.

10

Proper Spiritual Authority

I n your moments of pure bliss when you are on cloud nine with God, you must look out for the attacks that will try to come your way. In this chapter, I will let you in on one of the most character developing and devastating parts of my adult life after coming to God. I share this as a way of giving you the tools you need to stay vigilant and to protect your relationship with God—even from those who claim to be His followers.

When Leaders Fail Us

I had become a new creation. "Therefore, if anyone is in Christ, he is a new creation. The old has passed away; behold, the new has come" (2 Corinthians 5:17). I started talking differently, and I wanted my words to be pleasing to God. I started dressing differently. I felt beautiful and wanted to dress that way for my God. I also began to see into the spirit realm and to speak prophetically.

Since I had now stepped into my calling and was walking in God fully, the pastor of the church in which I got saved took me under his wing and began to mentor me. He gave me books to study, he began to counsel me and he often prayed for me. He now respected this once "street girl." He even asked me to pray and share periodically with the congregation. I was told that others were jealous because I was seemingly becoming the pastor's favorite.

This was my first experience in a Christian church, so I went with the flow and naïvely believed everything the pastor and his wife said. I felt some of the female leaders having resentment toward me, but I had been so used to people envying me that I ignored it. In my heart I knew I was genuine, and I wanted to continue to grow in my relationship with God. I thought that meant I had to get on the inside with His chosen people whom I considered my spiritual mother and father.

Have you been tempted to get close to those in church leadership because you believe that a friendship with them would somehow enhance your status with God? This is a trick of Satan who tries to use a worldly way of thinking to destroy a believer. In the world, we are taught that getting ahead is about who you know. Christianity is not about knowing the most successful, established people in Christianity, but rather knowing the Maker of the people. I am now a pastor's wife and, believe me, we are working out our salvation with fear and trembling just as everybody else is.

I was taught that my calling was linked to the church in which I was saved, and I was taught that this particular church was where my anointing from God came. They forbade people from leaving the church, and if someone did, they denounced him or her. I was also taught to fight off Satan and all of his traps by cutting off everyone and everything that was influenced by the enemy. I might have needed that kind of fire and brimstone message to help me gain a fear of God, but it took years for me to undo a lot of the funky doctrine that was ingrained in me. More on that later.

Although the pastor taught me how to take authority over the devil, he also instilled in me a great fear when it came to everything and everyone around me. To this congregation, everyone could have a potential demon, and everything could be a trap from the devil. I became very dependent on the pastor to help me make decisions in my life. If I was going to travel somewhere, I would run it by the pastor. If I wanted to reach out to a new friend, I would run it by the pastor. I looked for some sort of guidance from the "man of God," as we all called him. Have you ever relied on anyone so much that you found yourself seeking his or her approval and opinion for everything? When you do, it really affects your ability to go to God, your first love (see Revelation 2:4).

After five years of attending this church, I had finally gained the approval of my spiritual parents—or that is what I thought. Everything came crashing down, however, after church one Sunday. The pastor's wife, whom I had loved dearly and even looked to as the ultimate example of a godly woman, called me in to her office. We were joined by the youth pastor, who was another woman of God I esteemed highly. In that setting, she accused me of the unthinkable. She said she believed that I had engaged in an inappropriate relationship with her husband, and she said that she had proof.

Initially, I laughed. I honestly thought she was joking. That is how insane her claims were to me. My laughter turned quickly to sadness when I realized she was 100 percent serious. She accused me of having led on her husband, who was over forty years my senior. She was twenty years younger than he was, and I believe she was extremely insecure about losing him to another woman. I had no knowledge of that until after the incident. She pulled out screenshots that she had asked another leader from the church to take. She had videos of the times that I happened to have held the pastor's hands in a prayer circle while the congregation held hands and prayed. In her mind, this was proof that there had been inappropriate behavior.

At that point I saw the hatred in her eyes toward me. The devil had convinced her of this sick narrative. I began to weep and told her that the devil wanted her to believe this lie. She snapped out of her anger-driven deception and came back to herself. She said that she believed me, but that she still believed her husband had developed an unhealthy relationship with me. The whole time, I looked at my youth pastor hoping she would vouch for my character. Even though I could see in her eyes that she felt bad for me, she did not stand up for me.

That was the day I allowed someone to break my spirit. I had grown up in the hood, been through hell and back at home and out of the home, experienced heartbreak, and experienced my dreams come crashing down, but none of those things had broken my spirit. Have you ever allowed something to affect you so much that you nearly did not recover? "For where your treasure is, there your heart will be also" (Matthew 6:21). Whatever we put before God will show us eventually where it stands in relation to the one who created it.

The people that I esteemed highly were flawed humans, as I was, but I had never considered that reality until their flaws hurt me deeply. I had been looking to this woman as a spiritual mother but could never understand why she was always distant. On that day, I realized that her distance was because of the deep animosity she had in her heart for me. I was so naïve that I did not think hate was possible from such a godly person. From that day forward I was no longer allowed to go to the pastor for mentoring, prayer or guidance. I was even afraid to look at him.

I continued attending church because I thought that I could not leave. I was determined to help the pastor's wife see that I was not a threat to her, so I began to serve her. What I did not realize was that I was losing myself in the process. I felt that I had disappointed this woman of God, and because of that, my times dancing on the moon with Jesus became a distant memory. I was blindsided by the accusation and was left shattered with absolutely no support from anyone in the church. I did not want to discourage my family from pursuing their faith by sharing all of the details; therefore, I put my head down and simply kept going to church.

Due to the leading of the pastors, I had cut off most of my unsaved friends, so I did not have any friends to talk to. My older sister was the one who reminded me that I go to church for God and not for people. That advice helped me to press on and keep looking to God. If it was not for the amazing personal relationship that I had experienced previously with God, my new faith would not have survived. I would have run far back into the arms of the world. It is important to establish your own relationship with God, because if you do not, you will not be rooted enough to withstand the trials of life.

Abuse of Authority

A tragic incident like this does not happen without many things going wrong. Let me break down what I see as the faults of each party. To begin with, the leadership in the church did not represent their positions well. The Bible instructs that those who teach the church are held to a higher standard. "Not many of you should become teachers, my brothers, for you know that we who teach will be judged with greater strictness" (James 3:1).

I believe that I should never have been mentored solely by the male pastor of the church. He was the only one who invested in my spiritual development. And while he never once was inappropriate with me or flirted with me, I should have noticed the red flags. One red flag was that he snuck Christian books to me during the service. He was not operating in full transparency, and that gave place for the enemy to create a false narrative. "Abstain from all appearance of evil" (1 Thessalonians 5:22 KJV). I think this truth is why Paul taught that older women are to teach and train the younger women (see Titus 2:3–5).

The female/male dynamic has always been tricky when that dynamic is outside of marriage. The Bible shares all throughout Scripture of the many men of God who fell into sin with women, including David, Solomon, Samson and Abraham.

The late Billy Graham kept strict rules in order to safeguard his marriage. One of them was that he would never be alone with anyone of the opposite sex.[1] He understood the importance of making sure his wife felt secure about his

1. Billy Graham, *Just As I Am* (New York: HarperCollins, 1997).

integrity. Leaders must use wisdom. If you are seeking counsel or mentorship from a leader, I would advise strongly you use wisdom as well. Do not give the enemy any room to allow rumors or lies to start. By all means, that does not mean that you should go around being suspicious of every member of the opposite sex, but you should place proper boundaries around yourself to avoid giving the devil an opening.

Another issue that came from the poor mishandling of the leadership was how the co-pastor, the wife, treated me. She was suspicious and angry with me because of her own feelings of envy. I honestly had no idea what I had been summoned to her for, but by the time I left her office I felt as David must have felt while he was on the run because King Saul wanted his head. I was a young ignorant believer, and her words crushed my spirit.

As believers, we cannot allow the lies of the enemy to take us that far. Paul prayed against false thoughts. He said, "We destroy arguments and every lofty opinion raised against the knowledge of God, and take every thought captive to obey Christ" (2 Corinthians 10:5). Had she taken her thoughts captive to obey Christ, the Holy Spirit would have led her into the truth.

I was in my early twenties and was on fire for Christ. After that encounter, however, it was as if a bucket of water had been poured over me, and I was left to burn out. Jesus warns His followers to be careful about causing young people to stumble. "Whoever causes one of these little ones who believe in me to sin, it would be better for him to have a great millstone fastened around his neck and to be drowned in the depth of the sea" (Matthew 18:6). I was ignorant in my understanding, but everything was dealt with so poorly by

the leadership—and I was so hurt by that poor leadership—
that I could have walked away from Christ. It was only because of the grace of God that my faith survived.

Destroyed for Lack of Knowledge

Now for where I went wrong. Since this was my first experience in a Christian church and I had experienced such supernatural encounters there, I truly believed that it was the only
place on the planet where I would be able to access God the
way I did. As I began to read the Bible, I learned that God
shares His glory with no one. While the pastor always said
that glory belonged to God only, I observed that he fed into
the praise of men. Even though he taught the congregation
never to praise him for the move of God, I believe that things
changed because he did not live out those beliefs.

I also enjoyed having a spiritual father figure, because I
had not felt a strong patriarchal bond for some time. I took
pride in being called someone's spiritual daughter. It felt
like when you visit your supportive grandpa and he tells you
that you can conquer anything and fulfill any dream. That
voice becomes a driving force in your life, and you cannot
wait until you see your wise old grandpa again to get your
encouragement tank filled. I needed encouragement, and it
came from the pastor. Eventually, the list of people I loved
the most included God, those pastors (a close second) and
then family and friends.

Instead of going directly to God for advice, I always asked
the pastor first. I tried to have a relationship with his wife,
but she always avoided me. Her husband and the youth
pastor were all I had. As you look through your list, how

close is God to anyone else? I would work on making a clear distinction between that person and God, because no one should come even close to the One who put breath in our lungs. Psalm 146:3 warns us not to put our trust in people, "in whom there is no salvation."

The Bible warns repeatedly that we should not put our confidence in mere mortals. I did not heed that warning, because I had received no real knowledge of that truth. Instead, I heard Bible passages about how we were to honor the man of God and the prophet of the house. The pastor's favorite story in the Bible must have been the one about how Elisha served and followed Elijah, because that is what I heard repeatedly (see 2 Kings 2). It was social conditioning. We were taught that we would receive the pastor's mantle to heal the sick, to prophesy and to see and hear God if we served under him as Elisha had Elijah.

I also grew up in a Catholic church, where it was my understanding that we were to go to the priest for every spiritual inquiry. As a child, I did not know that we had direct access to God. The apostle Paul references this when he says, "This was according to the eternal purpose that he has realized in Christ Jesus our Lord, in whom we have boldness and access with confidence through our faith in him" (Ephesians 3:11–12). Jesus became our mediator between God and men. Another man is not to be our mediator.

I got caught in a cycle of trying to impress the spiritual leaders. I believed that if I could impress them, then it meant I was doing well in God's eyes, too. The Bible speaks against that specifically. "For am I now seeking the approval of man, or of God? Or am I trying to please man? If I were still trying to please man, I would not be a servant of Christ" (Galatians

1:10). I truly loved God and had devoted my life fully to Him, but because of my ignorance, I had competing affections. I wanted the pastors to love me and approve of me, and I had made that goal the same as pleasing God. People's opinions of you do not affect what God thinks about you. Working or serving in ministry does not earn you a spot in heaven. "He saved us, not because of works done by us in righteousness, but according to his own mercy, by the washing of regeneration and renewal of the Holy Spirit" (Titus 3:5).

The Holy Spirit Is the Best Spiritual Authority

After I was accused by the co-pastor, I hung my head down and tried everything I could to prove to her that I was no threat. In the process, I took my eyes off of the incredible one-on-one moments I had been having with God. I felt that He was probably as disappointed in me as she had been. When she interrogated me that day in her office, I told her that I had no idea that anything I was doing or saying could have been considered inappropriate. She told me that I could not use that excuse for everything. I thought to myself, *But how would I know unless someone teaches me?*

Instead of looking for people to teach me, I should have been looking to the Word of God. I should have been asking the Holy Spirit to teach me how to navigate and operate in a church setting within the Body of Christ. Jesus taught, "The Helper, the Holy Spirit, whom the Father will send in my name, he will teach you all things and bring to your remembrance all that I have said to you" (John 14:26). If I had done as Timothy directs, I would have received godly wisdom along with the supernatural experiences I had been encountering. "Study to shew thyself approved unto God, a workman that needeth not to be ashamed, rightly dividing the word of truth" (2 Timothy 2:15 KJV). It does not matter how spiritual you are; if you lack wisdom, the enemy will use that lack against you to pop your holy bubble. That is what happened to me.

My lack of wisdom resulted in my spending a year of my life in total bondage to the insecurities of another woman. I do not blame her. I gave her that spiritual authority over me. Because I did, her opinion had too much power over my spiritual life. I was stuck between a rock and a hard place when I should have been standing on Christ, the solid rock. I esteemed men too highly, and God is a jealous God. He shares His glory with no one. No one should take the place of His voice and authority over the life of His children—not even a church.

We belong to God. We do not belong to a specific church or denomination. There is only one Church in His eyes, and that is the Body of Christ. "For where two or three are gathered in my name, there am I among them" (Matthew 18:20). Now, do not get me wrong. I am not encouraging people to forsake going to church or not to respect those in leadership of the church. "Obey your leaders and submit to them, for they are keeping watch over your souls, as those who will have to give an account" (Hebrews 13:17). I am talking specifically about an abusive church situation where those in leadership do not fear God. In my situation, they used their power to usurp authority over their subordinates.

After the accusations and trauma, I was not nursed back into health by the church. Instead, I was left for dead. I felt betrayed by my spiritual parents and all of the leaders in the church who knew what had happened. They all left me to figure out how to get back up. I felt as if one moment I was with my platoon fighting side by side in a war, and the next moment they turned around, shot at me and left me wounded on the ground to bleed out.

Has an occurrence with a Christian ever made you want to turn away from Christ? That is the enemy's number one goal when it comes to hurt that people in the church cause. It is in those times that you have to remember to separate God from those who represent Him. That is when you must remember the experiences, both big and small, that you have had with Him. You should remember those moments where you know it was nothing or no one else but God who could have come through for you.

The enemy wanted to use all I had been through as an opportunity to destroy me. He forgot completely one major detail, though. God and I had history, and there was no way I was letting go of that. Though my spirit was broken, I had enough fight in me to attempt to crawl back into my Savior's arms. I remembered how faithful He had been to me throughout my life. I crawled as far as I could, and then God sent me a lifeline.

Mr. Wonderful

In this season of my life I learned what it was like to be on the performance treadmill of church. I attended church and served in the worship and youth ministries. I did that routine on repeat. I was not growing spiritually, because I was afraid that if I did, I would cause a stir in the church again. In this time of spiritual numbness, Satan began to lay traps for me.

After three years of no contact, my ex-fiancé, and first love, reached out and wanted to catch up. I was broken and vulnerable, and I really needed a friend. I obliged. When we met, he said everything I had wanted to hear three years prior. I felt so safe with him that I shared with him about my heartache with the church. He was kind and supportive, and he expressed that he hoped we could rekindle the bond we had always shared deeply.

One thing had changed for me, however. Although I was broken and disillusioned, I was still a new creation in Christ. I no longer made decisions impulsively. I ran everything through the filter of God. As my ex talked his way persuasively back into my heart, the Spirit of God living in me warned me to stay away. After hours of talking and catching up about everything we had missed, I told him I did not feel a peace about pursuing things again. We went our separate ways. Less than a week later God sent the man who would become my husband.

It was Sunday at church, and I was leading worship as I did every weekend. During that period of time, I usually led worship with my eyes closed. I did this so that I could focus only on Jesus and not on the pain I had endured in the church. This Sunday, though, there was a young man in the crowd I had not seen before. I noticed him because of the way he looked at me. He was staring at me. As he watched me worship, it was as if he could see me deeper than anyone else ever had. God had granted him access to watch my one-on-one adoration of the King in its truest form, and he was mesmerized.

I had been in front of crowds since I had been a kid and had performed in stadiums of thousands. Never once had anyone ever looked at me the way this young man did. After worship, I took my seat. The pastor proceeded to call all the single women in the church up to the front to pray for their futures. I was single, but I had no interest in finding love. I wanted Jesus to remain the center of my affections. Because of this, and because I regularly avoided every interaction with the pastor after the drama, I ignored the pastor's call. He called me up to the altar anyway.

After I walked up begrudgingly, I remember feeling this tension in my back that made me turn around. It was as if the entire church had parted in two and all I could see was the new church attendee. After I realized that he could see me, I turned back around quickly and heard, *That is your husband.* That idea could not have been farther from my thoughts, so I shook it off and talked myself out of what happened. Then again, as clear as my internal thoughts could sound, I heard, *That is your husband.* Moments later, the pastor came over and prayed an oddly specific prayer about the man who was to be my future husband. His petitions were things that I had told God privately about who my husband would have to be if it was God's will for me to be married.

After the service, I was introduced to the young man named Renn. Because of what I had experienced at the altar, I greeted him and then ran for my life. In the weeks that followed, I could not get Renn out of my mind. I figured this had to be a distraction from the enemy. I did not want to think about anyone more than I thought about God, so I prayed day and night. I even prayed spiritual warfare prayers against my curiosity about him. My thoughts did not go away, however. One day, I was headed to church and talking to God about Renn, and I heard Him say that I should share with Renn that I was interested in pursuing a friendship. Bold, huh?

The last time I had a crush on someone had been when I was twelve. I also had never had to be the one to tell the guy that I was interested in him. I felt extremely out of my element. Sure enough, as I got to church early that day so did Renn and his family. He and I crossed paths in the church hallway during a time when it was just the two of us. Keep in mind, he had not the slightest idea that I even thought about him. His mother had given him my number to call me after the first day we met, but he had not called. As we were speaking, he explained that he had not called because he had gotten out of the military recently and was planning on moving to his home country, Grenada, to grow out his beard and learn more of the Bible.

I bluntly replied, "I already feel like I'll be missing out on something." His eyes opened wide, and that night he called. The next day we had our first date. Before the night was over, we held hands and prayed together. I again heard from God. I heard the Holy Spirit say, *Treasure him.* As time passed, and after receiving several confirmations that we were meant to be husband and wife, he decided to stay in New York. This love story is an entire book within itself so I will leave it at that. Seven months later we were married. God's hand was in it, and He did not want my fear of happiness or my lack of trust in people to get in the way of the person He had for me.

Had I rekindled the romance with my former boyfriend, I would have missed out on what God had in store for me. The enemy sent the decoy just before God sent the real thing. I often describe this near-miss as if I were at a train station. If I had been distracted entertaining my past, I could have missed the train that would have set me on course for my future. Such a scary feeling. It is important that you follow the leading of God. Choosing to marry my husband, despite the objections from some in the church and some from family, is what shifted the trajectory of my life.

Marriage helped me come back to myself. My confidence returned, and I felt comfortable in my own skin. I was happily married. I believed that I did not have to worry about offending the co-pastor anymore because I was a married woman. I imagined that her husband would now be a spiritual father to both my husband and me. The devil, however, had other ideas. He would have none of it.

That is when I discovered that the issue had never been my relationship with my pastor, but rather, the issue had been walking in my full power and authority in God. The enemy wanted to silence my voice. But God was working all of this for my good. Have you ever noticed that as soon as you start stepping into your call all hell breaks loose? Well, that is because it is breaking loose! The enemy of your soul does not want you to succeed, and he definitely does not want you to tap into your supernatural power. When that happens, he loses his grip on you.

The accuser of the brethren, as he is referred to in Revelation 12:10, was at it again with me in that church. This time it was public. At this stage in my Christian walk, I was leading the congregation into worship regularly. Some of my immediate family—my mom, brother, paternal sister and nephew—had given their hearts to Jesus and now attended church with me. I had also led many of my friends to Christ, and they attended with me as well.

This particular Sunday, per the co-pastor's request, the portion of the service when I was to have led worship was canceled. She proceeded to make an example of me in front of everyone in attendance. Other than my husband, who had to work that day, this included my family members and all of the youth ministry whom I had won to Jesus. As the co-pastor proceeded to speak against me, I just sat in my chair shaking. In between my sister's sobs, she pled with me to leave the church and go home with her immediately.

I was stunned and could not even move. I had no idea what to do. After the service, I left with my family and prayed for instructions from God about how to respond to that type of character assassination. While in my time of prayer, the Lord told me to be silent, to set my face like flint and to allow Him to vindicate me. That is what I did. Old Jeannie from the block would have handled this very differently, but the Holy Spirit tempered me and gave me the grace to endure.

Once my husband caught wind of everything that happened, he called a meeting with the leaders. God had clearly given him different instructions, because he set everyone straight. He confronted the pastor who had allowed his wife to attack all of us publicly and take control over a church service that was supposed to be unto God. Compared to the first time that I was attacked like this, my experience was very different. I now had my husband as a spiritual covering, and not the pastors who had been trying to break my spirit.

A few weeks later we were kicked out of the church. This was the same church that taught the congregation that those who ever left would lose their salvation and be condemned. They continued to slander me and my husband, but we knew God was with us. In reality, it was God rescuing us from a really bad situation. Our rejection by the people of the church was surely God's protection, and we became better because of it. This experience caused us to mature in God quickly and learn how to lead others to seek God's guidance during a crisis. It was also a very powerful testimony of what God had done in my life. Old me would have handled the situation very differently, to say it nicely, but because of the transformation that had taken place, I was able to be Christlike amid the injustice.

Even before everything went down the second time, I knew we were not supposed to be in that church. In your personal walk with God, you must be in a church where you are being nurtured and encouraged spiritually to do what God has called you to do. For a long time, I had known I had not been growing in God, but I stayed and gave those leaders spiritual authority over me—which they abused. God kept me there to meet my husband, but after I was married, my season in that church was over. Sadly, I ignored that fact until I was forced to leave.

My advice is that if God has been prompting you concerning your spiritual covering, pray and fast, seek counsel from other believers outside of your respected circle and ask God to lead you. Being obedient to His leading is better than staying somewhere that will lead to spiritual death.

What Do I See?

1. In what ways has the enemy used situations to try to break your spirit?
2. What false doctrines or beliefs have you been exposed to in a Christian setting that were the rules or beliefs of people?
3. To what things or people have you given too high esteem?
4. Who are those people that God uses to help you up when the enemy attacks you?

5. How has rejection from others served as God's protection in your life?

What Can I Learn?

- Do not put your full trust in people.
- The opinions of others do not define your reputation with God.
- Study the Scriptures for yourself and allow the Holy Spirit to be your greatest teacher.
- The enemy often sends a decoy before God sends the real treasure. Rely on God's leading.
- God always sends a lifeline. Be sure not to miss it.
- Satan's goal is to stop you from walking in full confidence in God. Do not dim your light.

Scriptures for Meditation

Colossians 3:2 KJV
Set your affection on things above, not on things on the earth.

1 Thessalonians 5:22 KJV
Abstain from all appearance of evil.

2 Timothy 2:15 KJV
Study to shew thyself approved unto God, a workman that needeth not to be ashamed, rightly dividing the word of truth.

Galatians 1:10

For am I now seeking the approval of man, or of God? Or am I trying to please man? If I were still trying to please man, I would not be a servant of Christ.

1 Timothy 2:5–6

For there is one God, and there is one mediator between God and men, the man Christ Jesus, who gave himself as a ransom for all, which is the testimony given at the proper time.

Prayer and Declaration

Dear Lord, I have been hurt in the church. Help me to forgive those who claim to be from You, and help me to look to You, my true spiritual authority. May I never allow anyone to break my spirit or interfere in my relationship with You. Holy Spirit, teach me Your Word and Your ways and help me to remember Your goodness in times of devastation and heartbreak. Keep me in a healthy church that loves and serves people as Jesus did. May this always be my declaration: Who shall separate me from the love of Christ? Shall tribulation, or distress, or persecution, or famine, or nakedness, or danger, or sword? No, in all these things I am more than a conqueror through Him who loves me. For I am sure that neither death nor life, nor angels nor rulers, nor things present nor things to come, nor powers, nor height nor depth, nor anything else in all creation, will be able to separate me from the love of God in Christ Jesus our Lord (see Romans 8:35–39). In Jesus' name, Amen.

11

Fighting from Victory

n every one of these chapters I have shown you how both God and the enemy were present in my life even while I was unaware. My hope has been to paint for you a picture of a very real spiritual realm. Before my spiritual eyes were opened, I had never noticed that there were supernatural things at work. Let's face it, most people live life focused only on what they can see.

Now that you have gone through these chapters and have reflected on your own supernatural encounters and occurrences, I would like to tell you how to remain in a place of victory over the evil one and his relentless attacks. There are many spiritual activities you can do to help yourself overcome the enemy of your soul—fasting, spiritual warfare, attending revival services, calling on the angels from heaven, etc.—but I have found five simple spiritual practices that have been extremely effective in helping me fight from a place of victory.

Keep Your Eyes Open

Begin by being honest with yourself. How often do you live your life and forget that there is a spiritual battle being fought around you that is intent on derailing you from your purpose? How often do you read the Bible through the lens of the supernatural instead of looking to find practical things you can use on a daily basis? The price that Jesus paid to rid the world of its demonic pollution should never be taken for granted, and part of the process of honoring His sacrifice is remembering that what is happening in you is tied to a greater battle for your eternal fate.

John the Baptist said, "Behold, the Lamb of God, who takes away the sin of the world" (John 1:29). Up until this point the Israelites had sacrificed lambs to God, because the bloodshed of the innocent animal was a sign of life and would provide purification for the people of God. John made this powerful declaration before he baptized Jesus, signifying that the Savior had come to absolve our sins.

Jesus did that once and for all on the cross. He came to deliver the Word of God and was the Word who became flesh and dwelt among us. He came to restore all people to their God, and He died so that we could all experience what He prayed for when He said, "On earth as it is in heaven" (Matthew 6:10). Humanity had once been united with God in the Garden of Eden. In that glorious place heaven and earth overlapped. Men were given access to the garden until the evil one manipulated Adam and Eve to sin. Since then, God's intent remains to reconcile us to Himself.

"He himself bore our sins in his body on the tree, that we might die to sin and live to righteousness. By his wounds you have been healed" (1 Peter 2:24). If you do not look at that verse through the lens of the supernatural, you will miss the good news that His sacrificial death and resurrection allowed Him to leave us the Holy Spirit. The presence of God is how we now experience heaven on earth. His presence that we experience in us as a spirit-filled believer is nothing but supernatural.

I remember when I first saw the movie *The Passion of the Christ*. I had not fully surrendered my life to God and was sad to see Jesus tortured and killed on the cross. Upon his death, the ambiguous character who played the devil shouted in agony because he had once and for all been defeated by Jesus.

To the natural eye, it looked as if the enemy had won, because Jesus had been tortured and killed by the people He came to save. But the spiritual implications took place in an unseen battle. You and I can hold onto that victory whenever the enemy of our soul tries to use shame, guilt or condemnation against us.

Jesus' death means we have victory over the powers of darkness. His sacrifice and the shedding of His sinless blood disarmed those demonic powers and authorities in high places who are constantly gunning for us to forfeit eternity with God. Jesus made a spectacle of the evil one in His public death as He triumphed over darkness. He "gave himself for our sins to deliver us from the present evil age, according to the will of our God and Father" (Galatians 1:4).

Love as if You Have Never Been Hurt

After being radically saved, drastically transformed and tragically hurt, I felt the devil gunning for my victory. He wanted me to doubt everything and turn from God. The hurt that I felt toward the people I had trusted kept replaying in my mind and heart. The sense of abandonment made me feel hopeless.

One morning, I had a dream in which all the hurt I had experienced and the pain I had felt was so real that I was awakened. I fell to my knees immediately and began to weep. I proceeded to tell God how hurt and betrayed I felt. I talked with Him about everything I had gone through, and I finally allowed myself to feel it all. My husband knelt next to me and consoled me.

That day, I learned God wants our pain so that He can trade it for His joy. Following that emotional purge, I asked God how I could ever forgive those who had hurt me. The Holy Spirit responded by saying, *I want you to love as if you have never been hurt.* The enemy had given me a list of excuses I could use to make me feel as if I were fighting a losing battle, but God reminded me of my most powerful weapon: love.

It is important to release offenses or hurts that keep us from walking in full victory. To help with the releasing process, I recommend that you write all of your thoughts and emotions out, that you spend time in prayer and wait until the Holy Spirit uproots what you are feeling, or that you go to therapy, where someone can help you uncover the deep-rooted blockages in your life. Regardless of the method, what is important is that you clear yourself from anything that creates an alliance between you and the enemy.

Jesus told His followers, "A new commandment I give to you, that you love one another: just as I have loved you, you also are to love one another. By this all people will know that you are my disciples, if you have love for one another" (John 13:34–35). When we stop operating out of love, we can switch our allegiance unknowingly from God to the enemy. If you truly understand that love wins, why would you want to do that? The Word of God is clear that love is what conquers all, and the people of God are to walk in love. John shares why it is important that we keep bearing this fruit until the end.

> So we have come to know and to believe the love that God has for us. God is love, and whoever abides in love abides in God, and God abides in him. By this is love perfected with us, so that we may have confidence for the day of judgment, because as he is so also are we in this world. There is no fear in love, but perfect love casts out fear. For fear has to do with punishment, and whoever fears has not been perfected in love. We love because he first loved us. If anyone says, 'I love God,' and hates his brother, he is a liar; for he who does not love his brother whom he has seen cannot love God whom he has not seen. And this commandment we have from him: whoever loves God must also love his brother.
>
> 1 John 4:16–21

God wants us to abide in love so that we can be confident in the end. But how can we be confident and fight from a place of victory? We cannot lose sight of love. I have seen this firsthand. I have had natural battles in which Satan wanted to use things or people to throw me off course, but when I responded in love rather than the instinctual reaction of fear from which hatred is born, the chains were broken. I did not lose my faith or my peace for one second.

Everything God has done comes from a place of love. The Bible tells us that God is love (see 1 John 4:8), and that "God so loved the world, that he gave his only son" (John 3:16). His love was so great that He laid down His life for us even while we were still sinners and were rejecting Him. His love is everlasting, steadfast and much stronger than anything on the face of the planet. The following passage breaks down the type of love God is asking us to share with each other.

If I speak in the tongues of men and of angels, but have not love, I am a noisy gong or a clanging cymbal. And if I have prophetic powers, and understand all mysteries and all knowledge, and if I have all faith, so as to remove mountains, but have not love, I am nothing. If I give away all I have, and if I deliver up my body to be burned, but have not love, I gain nothing.

Love is patient and kind; love does not envy or boast; it is not arrogant or rude. It does not insist on its own way; it is not irritable or resentful; it does not rejoice at wrongdoing, but rejoices with the truth. Love bears all things, believes all things, hopes all things, endures all things. Love never ends. . . . So now faith, hope, and love abide, these three; but the greatest of these is love.

I Corinthians 13:1–13

The apostle Paul wrote of the battles that would come for believers, because he had firsthand experience with most of them. He tried to prepare those who would follow after his example.

In all these things we are more than conquerors through him who loved us. For I am sure that neither death nor life, nor angels nor rulers, nor things present nor things to come, nor powers, nor height nor depth, nor anything else in all creation, will be able to separate us from the love of God in Christ Jesus our Lord.

Romans 8:37–39

Every trial of life and every supernatural attack is included in the above passage. A revelation of God's love is necessary to be able to walk in that level of authority. I find myself holding onto these words every day as the world fights for my attention. The enemy uses temporal disappointments to try to rob me of the concept of everlasting love.

In All Things Be Thankful

Another tool to help keep you fighting is gratitude. Some of the happiest people in the world are those who live lives of thanksgiving in spite of their circumstances. An attitude of gratitude will keep you in a perpetual place of inner joy and peace.

My favorite chapter of the Bible is Colossians 3, because it offers practical guidelines for how to live this life in service to God and to each other. If you are anything like me and had no sense of godliness or godly behavior before coming to Jesus, then you will really appreciate this chapter, too.

Let the peace of Christ rule in your hearts, to which indeed you were called in one body. And be thankful. Let the word of Christ dwell in you richly, teaching and admonishing one another in all wisdom, singing psalms and hymns and spiritual songs, with thankfulness in your hearts to God. And whatever you do, in word or deed, do everything in the name of the Lord Jesus, giving thanks to God the Father through him.

Colossians 3:15–17

The author mentions thankfulness three different times, and he encourages the believer to serve God in the posture of gratitude. I have learned that when I remain in a position of gratitude, I remain in a healthy place mentally, emotionally and spiritually.

I cannot tell you how many times I have heard people I mentor say, "I just want to know what God's will is for my life." People want to open the Bible and see things such as "Jeannie, God wants you to create an album and travel the world sharing His good news with the world. Do not worry. He will supply all of your needs and will use your testimony to bring many people to Himself."

I get it. That might seem the easier thing for some, but it is also extremely bland. It would, in turn, cause us all to want to manipulate how His will for us ends up. Ultimately, His will for us is that we rejoice. "Rejoice always, pray without ceasing, give thanks in all circumstances; for this is the will of God in Christ Jesus for you" (1 Thessalonians 5:16–18). I believe that being appreciative leads to a lifestyle of prayer and rejoicing. The enemy hates that kind of life. If you enjoy your life regardless of what comes your way, he cannot destroy you.

My best days with God have been the seasons of my life in which I have been able to say, "Thank you, God, for blessing me far greater than I deserve." I now live in Orlando, Florida, with my husband. I am more excited about God than I have ever been, and my personal time with Him has been deeper than ever. Due to God's grace, we own a house and a car, and we have two precious dogs that we love dearly. We have a ministry with a group of incredible people with whom we share life in Christ and friendship. My parents, brothers and sisters all love Jesus, are in good health and are blessed. We were led to a church that covers both my husband and I as we travel the world speaking, singing and encouraging others to know Jesus. I work in Christian media; I also work on a TV show that allows me to lift up the name of Jesus, and I am now an author. None of this was planned. The only part that I have played is that I have been grateful for everything I have ever received, and I have offered all things back to Him. He did the rest.

My biggest battle in life now, despite all of my blessings, is remaining content. I know that this job of remaining content is where many of us give in to the attacks of the devil. If Adam and Eve had been content with all that God had freely given them, they would not have been deceived by the serpent. Their focus would have been on the glory of heaven meeting earth.

Many times, I have given room for the enemy because I was not in a posture of thanksgiving. Instead, I was feeling sorry for myself. As a result, the attacks came rolling in. Since my heart was not right, my armor was completely off. We must learn how to constantly assess the state of our armor.

Use Your Spiritual Weapons

My husband and my best friend are former soldiers, one a United States airman and the other an army special agent. I have learned quite a bit about what happens as soldiers prep for war. First, they head to basic training, or boot camp, where they work on their foundations. Once they complete that intensive course, they head to special training. It is here that they hone their skills in whatever their specialty will be. After this process is complete, the soldiers are assigned to units where they join with their platoon. While in active duty they continue training and working on their specialty. Then the moment comes when soldiers are deployed for war. This means they are sent into a place of combat.

I look at this process as something very similar to what happens when we become Christians. We are enlisted automatically in the army of God. Whether people are believers or not, they are a part of a full-on war for their souls that is waging in the spiritual realm. When we enlist in the army of God we are to train for how to respond to that war. All of us have to come to the place where we decide willingly to serve on God's side of the war.

Salvation is our foundation, and connecting to a body of believers and attending church is what we do to train in our faith and strengthen ourselves. When the battle comes, we cannot roll over and allow the enemy to wreak havoc and take over everything. What a disaster it would be if our military soldiers spent their time training and learning their specialties, but when the battle came, they allowed the enemy to pummel them and take over all they had been trained to safeguard.

The military calls that a dereliction of duty, and it is highly condemned. We as the army of Christ do it all the time, however, when we allow the cares of life to rob us of the victory that we have in Christ Jesus. The difference between a physical war and a spiritual war is that we know who will triumph in the end. "Thanks be to God, who in Christ always leads us in triumphal procession" (2 Corinthians 2:14). In Jesus, if we do not faint, we will march onward to victory.

We are not to retreat on the day of battle. We are to dress for battle with our spiritual armor and stand firm as instructed (see Ephesians 6). "With God we shall do valiantly; it is he who will tread down our foes" (Psalm 108:13). God is only asking us to prepare for and endure within the battle. "The LORD your God is he who goes with you to fight for you against your enemies, to give you the victory" (Deuteronomy 20:4).

We are in a battle, and we are all soldiers. We can choose to go into the battle defenseless with doors open to the enemy's attacks, or we can be covered by the blood of Jesus, suited for battle with the armor of God on and standing against the enemy. Our brave soldiers do not train for war only to allow the enemy to defeat them when the battle comes. They fight. We, too, as spiritual soldiers, must do the same. We fight the good fight of faith!

Believe the Truth

In order to stay in a place of victory, you must believe the truth about both yourself and God. The two go hand in hand. If you believe that Jesus saved you and overcame evil, but you loathe yourself, you do not really believe He overcame evil. Only the devil would promote such lies. Also, if you think you are the greatest creation on earth but do not believe the truth of the Gospel, then you are riddled with arrogance and pride. These will also lead to your downfall.

Looking back at my life I have had moments of both. Most recently, I experienced several deaths in my womb. I experienced what the medical community calls *missed miscarriage*. This is when a baby begins to grow but then, with little explanation, it stops growing. These events challenged both my self-worth and my faith. I had my Job moments when I wrestled with God about it and wondered why He would allow such pain and disappointment. In the end, I came to the conclusion, "The LORD gave, and the LORD has taken away; blessed be the name of the LORD" (Job 1:21).

I still had moments where I questioned myself, my usefulness, my womanhood and even my purpose. In those moments, God whispered to me that what He is doing in me is greater than what is happening to me. I am able to look at this natural trauma in a spiritual way and see how it has paved a way for my husband and me to adopt and help provide safety for other children, even as we continue to cover my womb in prayer. The apostle Paul, inspired by the Holy Spirit, spoke of this.

> We do not lose heart. Though our outer self is wasting away, our inner self is being renewed day by day. For this light momentary affliction is preparing for us an eternal weight of glory beyond all comparison, as we look not to the things that are seen but to the things that are unseen. For the things that are seen are transient, but the things that are unseen are eternal.
>
> 2 Corinthians 4:16–18

Opening your spiritual eyes to see the unseen requires you to become aware of the truth of your life, the battle for your eternal salvation, and the promise of God who conquered sin, death, hell and the grave. I know my story is not over, and I also know the attack the enemy unleashed on my legacy must bow to the God I serve. That truth will not waver because of the promises of God, so I keep my focus on what is eternal.

How do you believe the truth about yourself and God when all kinds of attacks come against you? Jesus taught about this in a parable in which He used the example of a farmer sowing seeds. The seed falls along the path, on rocky ground, among thorns or on good soil.

> "Listen then to what the parable of the sower means: When anyone hears the message about the kingdom and does not understand it, the evil one comes and snatches away what was sown in their heart. This is the seed sown along the path. The seed falling on rocky ground refers to someone who hears the word and at once receives it with joy. But since they have no root, they last only a short time. When trouble or persecution comes because of the word, they quickly fall away. The seed falling among the thorns refers to someone who hears the word, but the worries of this life and the deceitfulness of wealth choke the word, making it unfruitful. But the seed falling on good soil refers to someone who hears the word and understands it. This is the one who produces a crop, yielding a hundred, sixty or thirty times what was sown."
>
> Matthew 13:18–23 NIV

We have a great deal available to us in this day and age to help us understand the Word of God, but our greatest tool is the Holy Spirit who leads us into all truth. The enemy wants the seeds of truth to fall away and not take root in us or to get choked up by the cares of this life. But becoming like Christ and understanding who we are in Him is a supernatural occurrence that is 100 percent the Holy Spirit's job.

Our part is to accept by faith and believe what God says is true about Himself and us. In order to believe these truths, we must fight off a three-fold enemy—the evil one, the memory of who we used to be without God and the distractions of this world. In order to do this, we must reject the lies we have believed that are contrary to God's Word. We must then replace them with what God says.

Jesus makes us whole. As we saw from His earthly example, He was so pure that when He touched others, they were made complete. At His resurrection, He assured His followers that by His Holy Spirit He would make His dwelling among us. In the Hebrew language, the word used translates as "temple." We must remain in the truth about our identity in God, and this truth will keep us walking in victory. The book of Revelation speaks of the final battle when Jesus will return as King and deal with evil forever. It tells us that He will vindicate those who have been faithful to Him (see Revelation 14; 16). Hold on to that truth and use it to encourage yourself to fight from a place of victory.

What Do I See?

1. What can you do to keep your spiritual eyes open?
2. How can you practice love in a greater way to help you stay in a place of victory?

3. What habits, people, thoughts or activities are blocking you from remaining in a place of victory?

4. How has discontentment led you into a place of defeat?

5. What kind of soil (from the parable we discussed) would you say you are presently?

6. In what ways will you adjust your thoughts, actions and emotions to stay in a place of victory?

What Can I Learn?

- Jesus' death on the cross conquered the enemy and triumphed over the powers of darkness.
- Love is the most powerful weapon we can use while in the battle.
- Love as if you have never been hurt, because love conquers all.
- Do not allow hatred or unforgiveness to create an alliance between you and the enemy.
- In all things be thankful, and you will remain in victory.
- Dress for battle and stand firm.
- Believe the truth about yourself and God. Reject the lies of the enemy and replace them with truth.
- The Holy Spirit leads you into all truth. All you have to do is believe it.
- God has provided us tools to use to fight the good fight of faith. Use them. We have the victory!

Scriptures for Meditation

Colossians 1:16

For by him all things were created, in heaven and on earth, visible and invisible, whether thrones or dominions or rulers or authorities—all things were created through him and for him.

Colossians 2:15 NKJV

Having disarmed principalities and powers, He made a public spectacle of them, triumphing over them in it.

Matthew 28:18

"All authority in heaven and on earth has been given to me."

Ephesians 1:19–21 NIV

That power is the same as the mighty strength he exerted when he raised Christ from the dead and seated him at his right hand in the heavenly realms, far above all rule and authority, power and dominion, and every name that is invoked, not only in the present age but also in the one to come.

James 4:7

Submit yourselves therefore to God. Resist the devil, and he will flee from you.

2 Corinthians 4:16–18

So we do not lose heart. Though our outer self is wasting away, our inner self is being renewed day by day. For this light momentary affliction is preparing for us an eternal weight of glory beyond all comparison, as we look not to the things that are seen but to the things that are unseen. For the things that are seen are transient, but the things that are unseen are eternal.

Prayer and Declaration

Heavenly Father, I thank You that in Christ Jesus we have the victory. God, I am grateful for Your Word, and I am grateful for Your Holy Spirit who leads us into all truth. I lay down everything that might be standing in the way of my walking in Your victory. Help me to love as if I have never been hurt. Help me to forgive, and help me to remember that Your sacrifice on the cross was enough to deliver me from all of the attacks of Satan. God, I pray that from this moment on I would renew my mind with Your truth and put on the armor of God. Please help me stand firm, knowing that in You I am triumphant. Help me to remain in this victory. May I use Your Word as my weapon and walk in that authority in You, Jesus. Thank you for defeating the enemy. My faith, my hope, my trust is in You. In Jesus' name, Amen.

12

How to Defeat Your Enemy

What is happening? With all that is going on in the world it is important to have discernment. As we have looked at my life in the previous chapters, I really hope that you have reflected on your life as well. In this final chapter, I want to zoom out and talk about the grand scheme of it all.

The Bible records the lives of generations of people, some of whom understood what was going on in the spiritual world and followed God's lead, and others who were asleep or missed His plan entirely. Each of those reactions had specific outcomes and had an impact on the future of all who followed them. A Christian's discernment determines the outcome of his or her life. It determines how he or she will react to what is happening around him or her.

What I have learned through my life's journey is that following God's lead is the only answer to everything that comes my way in life. When monumental things happen, such as global pandemics, natural disasters or war, we are sure to listen for instructions from those who govern us. That is great. We should be informed and ready to listen to guidance if applicable. More than that, however, we need to be focused on God. There is a colossal spiritual battle happening for the souls of every person. Seeking God is imperative.

Will You Respond to the Invitation?

As the days get darker, I find myself praying that I am able to stay sensitive to the supernatural temperature of the world. I would hate to miss God's instructions and be left behind. After all that Moses did to lead Israel out of slavery, he did not make it to the Promised Land because he did not follow God's instructions (see Deuteronomy 1; Numbers 20). In fact, all of Israel, except for Joshua and Caleb, missed it, because they were too concerned with what was happening in the natural. They missed the spiritual importance of their liberation completely. It is imperative that you know what is happening so that you respond the way God asks you to.

Jesus shared a few parables in which we see this happen. First is the story of the ten virgins found in Matthew 25. The ten virgins all knew that the wedding feast was happening, but only five of them kept their lamps burning with oil. The other five let their lamps burn out. By the time they got their lamps burning again, they had missed their opportunity to enter into the feast with the bridegroom. Jesus warns, "Watch therefore, for you know neither the day nor the hour" (verse 13). He encourages His followers to stay vigilant, alert and awake, because no one knows when the Day of Judgment will come.

Another parable that Jesus shared was about a banquet. This story is another example of a truly tragic instance for those who were invited and did not show up. Due to their lack of discernment, they missed their opportunity to taste of the goodness of God. They had no idea what was going to happen at that banquet, and the distractions in their lives caused them to miss the invitation from God.

"A man once gave a great banquet and invited many. And at the time for the banquet he sent his servant to say to those who had been invited, 'Come, for everything is now ready.' But they all alike began to make excuses. The first said to him, 'I have bought a field, and I must go out and see it. Please have me excused.' And another said, 'I have bought five yoke of oxen, and I go to examine them. Please have me excused.' And another said, 'I have married a wife, and therefore I cannot come.' So the servant came and reported these things to his master. Then the master of the house became angry and said to his servant, 'Go out quickly to the streets and lanes of the city, and bring in the poor and crippled and blind and lame.' And the servant said, 'Sir, what you commanded has been done, and still there is room.' And the master said to the servant, 'Go out to the highways and hedges and compel people to come in, that my house may be filled. For I tell you, none of those men who were invited shall taste my banquet.'"

Luke 14:16–24

Not being aware of what is happening around you will have a large impact on your eternal fate. As we see in the example above, not responding to God's beckoning will affect the generations who come after us. Over and over in Scripture we see moments where people had no idea of what was going on. Some of them missed the spiritual message being delivered in those moments, while others sought God for clarity or trusted Him through the uncertainty.

At Jesus' death, for example, some people wept while others cursed and shouted. Within the dramatic events of His death we get a glimpse of what happens when you have a revelation from God. The thief on the cross who was hanging next to the Savior of the world realized that God was beside him, and he asked to be with Jesus in paradise (see Luke 23:42). In that moment he was granted access to eternal life with God. In contrast, the centurion who guarded the crucifixion and those around him did not realize the majesty of who was on the cross until after His death. Upon Jesus' death there was an earthquake. The awe of this event opened the centurion's eyes and made him realize that Jesus was the Son of God (see Matthew 27:54).

Abraham and Sarah are another example of people in the Bible who had a relationship with God but missed what He was doing. They allowed the enemy to entice them into making their own plan. Abram, who is renamed Abraham, receives a promise from God that he will be the father of many nations (see Genesis 15). From his offspring will come kings and great nations. Abraham was 99 and his wife, Sarah, was quite old. They had believed that because of her age it would be impossible for her to conceive. Because of this, they came up with another plan. Sarah asked her Egyptian slave, Hagar, to get pregnant in her stead. Because Abraham and Sarah were not using their discernment or seeking God for

His instructions on how He was going to fulfill His promise, they contrived their own plan. Along with the baby that was born outside of God's best for Abraham and Sarah, an entire rebel nation was birthed.

The Lord again spoke to Abraham concerning having a child with Sarah (see Genesis 17:4–8). Three angels were sent to make it clear that Sarah would be the one who would conceive. It was out of that seed from which Jesus came. Abraham and Sarah's lack of discernment caused immediate difficulties for all involved, as well as caused generations of strife. I believe that it should not have taken that long for the people of God to have realized what He was saying.

Job is a man in the Bible who had all kinds of destruction leveled on him because the enemy had been given permission to test his faith (see Job 1:6–12). We get a glimpse of how he had no idea what was happening to him as he shared his confusion with God. "Why did you bring me out from the womb?" (Job 10:18). Through this account, we see that even when we are spiritually ignorant, if we refuse to sin and keep our focus and our praise on God, He protects us and gives us double for our trouble (see Job 42:10). Jesus is God, He loves you, He wants you to be upright and you should praise Him. Regardless of what comes against you, God will be with you.

Unfortunately for Judas Iscariot, a disciple of Jesus who walked with Him while He was on earth, he missed the point that Jesus had been trying to teach him. Satan was allowed to enter into Judas (see Luke 22:3–4). Had this disciple received a revelation of who Jesus really was, he would have resisted the enemy when he came to put the idea of betrayal into his heart (see John 13:2).

The devil told Judas to betray Jesus, which he did. He bit the bait immediately. Remember, Judas was someone who had walked with Jesus. While it is mind-boggling that he spent time with Jesus and still allowed himself to be tempted, how often do we take the deceiver's bait? How often do we give in to the temptation of the enemy instead of fighting back? We have to be sure that we are spiritually clear enough to hear from God and be able to respond to His leading.

Judas' story ended tragically with him hanging himself. We must not allow the enemy to trick us or rob us of our eternal standing with God. Just because you do not know what is happening does not mean that nothing is happening. In the spiritual realm something is always going on. Seek God and be informed. We have a choice, as Job did, to submit ourselves to God and resist the devil or to give in to the plan of the evil one.

Spiritual Senses

I used to think that defeating my personal battles with the enemy meant I had to yell, shout in my heavenly language, have someone lay hands on me or have someone douse me with anointing oil. While those things may have some effect, I now see that lasting spiritual deliverance actually hangs on our complete faith in Christ Jesus.

Let me break some things down for you. As believers in Christ we have spiritual senses: see, hear, taste, smell and touch. These senses are given to us from the Spirit of God to help us discern good and evil. It is up to us whether or not we activate them. I would also like to add our mind to that list, as it is worth focusing on. To some, the mind is considered the sixth sense.

Let's start there. The apostle Paul teaches that we are to have the mind of Christ. When we do, we will not reject the wisdom that comes from God.

> No one comprehends the thoughts of God except the Spirit of God. Now we have received not the spirit of the world, but the Spirit who is from God, that we might understand the things freely given us by God. And we impart this in words not taught by human wisdom but taught by the Spirit, interpreting spiritual truths to those who are spiritual. The natural person does not accept the things of the Spirit of God, for they are folly to him, and he is not able to understand them because they are spiritually discerned. The spiritual person judges all things, but is himself to be judged by no one. "For who has understood the mind of the Lord so as to instruct Him?" But we have the mind of Christ.
>
> 1 Corinthians 2:11–16

In order to understand the unseen things at work in our lives or the things that are happening in the world around us, we need the wisdom of God. How do we get that divine wisdom? We have to set our minds on God.

> For those who live according to the flesh set their minds on the things of the flesh, but those who live according to the Spirit set their minds on the things of the Spirit. For to set the mind on the flesh is death, but to set the mind on the Spirit is life and peace.
>
> Romans 8:5–6

How can we do that in such a distracted age? Well, we should be intentional about spending time with Him. You will make time for what you love. I used to believe the lie that people are too busy. I believed that they got a pass because of their important responsibilities. But when you put yourself in the shoes of the one being neglected, you see that people really will move heaven and earth to spend the time with someone or something they care about.

The issue is that people do not always see the importance of keeping their minds on Christ. This discipline is truly one of the most important things in the life of a Christian who hopes to be walking in the fullness of God. Your mind and thoughts are spiritual senses that you cannot live without when you are trying to discern good from evil or what is from God and what is not. "Be sober-minded; be watchful. Your adversary the devil prowls around like a roaring lion, seeking someone to devour" (1 Peter 5:8). This Scripture has always helped me to make sure my mind was never impaired by illegal drugs, medicine or alcohol.

I refuse to be lured away by the enemy because I am not in the right state of mind. Oppression and depression can also put you in an impaired state. What do you do when battling mental issues? I would say reach out to a trusted community of friends who will pray with you and over you. Open the Word of God, declare the truths of God over your life and believe them. The evil one cannot handle when someone proclaims Scripture and believes it, because then he has nothing to work with.

If what you are dealing with is a medical condition, seek the help you need. But still, remember God is Lord over medicine and a diagnosis. Choose to trust in Him above anything, committing your thoughts and mind to Him. "You keep him in perfect peace whose mind is stayed on you, because he trusts in you" (Isaiah 26:3).

Eyes

The next sense we should use is sight. I am sure that you have heard that the eyes are the window to the soul. I never knew that statement was actually inspired by the Scriptures until I began to delve into the Word of God for myself. Jesus illustrates wonderfully the importance of one's eyes in Luke 11. In order to decipher what is going on in the spiritual world through God's perspective, you have to be enlightened. He does not grant His spiritual vision to someone whose eyes have been darkened. Jesus shares what He thinks about the eyes of a person.

> "No one after lighting a lamp puts it in a cellar or under a basket, but on a stand, so that those who enter may see the light. Your eye is the lamp of your body. When your eye is healthy, your whole body is full of light, but when it is bad, your body is full of darkness. Therefore be careful lest the light in you be darkness. If then your whole body is full of light, having no part dark, it will be wholly bright, as when a lamp with its rays gives you light."
>
> Luke 11:33–36

How do you keep your eyes healthy? You must be careful about what you watch. I have seen in the spiritual realm since I was a child. Sadly, many of those years were spent seeing things I should not have, such things as demonic idols, spiritual feasts dedicated to the dead, violence, pornography and abuse. It was not until I was born again in Christ that I started to fill my eyes with things that were holy, righteous and pure.

What we look at in the natural affects what happens to us in the spiritual realm. The eye invites the spiritual realm into your body. Jesus taught, "But I say to you that everyone who looks at a woman with lustful intent has already committed adultery with her in his heart" (Matthew 5:28). He wanted to be clear that the eye is the lamp of the body, and what you look at affects the outcome of that light. "If your right eye causes you to sin, tear it out and throw it away. For it is better that you lose one of your members than that your whole body be thrown into hell" (verse 29). This is a warning to which we should take heed. If Jesus felt the need to be graphic in His example, then we should take seriously watching what we see with our eyes.

As a child, I was obsessed with horror films. My friends and I used to search the web for the goriest real-life accidents to study the carnage. Those images became ingrained in my mind and thoughts, and I am sure they lent to the years of nightmares that I had. I now look at photos of myself when I was younger and can see darkness in my eyes. I compared my first album cover to my most recent photos. My eyes, although they are still green, look different. I can see the light now, whereas before all I saw was the pain.

My mind and heart are now set on God. In place of the night terrors, I now see visions and have dreams from God. Some of the dreams are prophetic while others are warnings. That is why I believe it is important to both physically and spiritually take care of our eyes. "Open my eyes to see the wonderful truths in your instructions" (Psalm 119:18 NLT). This should be our prayer.

Ears

"He who has an ear, let him hear." Jesus said this phrase over and over during His time on the earth. Hearing is another important spiritual sense. The Scriptures are filled with verses about the importance of turning one's ears to God and His teachings. In order to get a revelation of where you are in the Lord and what is happening around you, you have to be able to hear Him. The Savior says, "My sheep hear my voice, and I know them, and they follow me. I give them eternal life, and they will never perish, and no one will snatch them out of my hand" (John 10:27–28).

If our ears are locked in to God, then we will not be swept away by the evil one.

> For the time is coming when people will not endure sound teaching, but having itching ears they will accumulate for themselves teachers to suit their own passions, and will turn away from listening to the truth and wander off into myths.
>
> 2 Timothy 4:3–4

Keeping your ears clear from the enemy's enticement should be a discipline within your spiritual routine. It is important to keep your spiritual senses heightened to what God is saying. What do you do when the world around you does not have an answer for what you are seeking? I lived through the beginning months of the global pandemic of COVID-19. Without having a cure in sight, many people died. No one had the answer. In those moments, I had the choice to listen to the news and the mass hysteria or to incline my ear to God and trust Him for my life, for the lives of my loved ones and for the future of my country. I received specific instructions from Him on what to do and what not to do. Because of that I was able to keep my peace. I was even able to offer advice and be a source of consultation and comfort to the people around me. Jesus talks about the negative effects of not listening or looking to Him.

"For this people's heart has grown dull, and with their ears they can barely hear, and their eyes they have closed, lest they should see with their eyes and hear with their ears and understand with their heart and turn, and I would heal them."

Matthew 13:15

The book of Proverbs breaks down the benefit of using our ears in this spiritual life. "An intelligent heart acquires knowledge, and the ear of the wise seeks knowledge" (Proverbs 18:15). Proverbs also tells us, "The ear that listens to life-giving reproof will dwell among the wise" (15:31).

Mouth

Oh boy, this is the sense that gets me in the most trouble! It is also a spiritual practice that comes with powerful authority. The words that come out of your mouth are like fire. If they are too hot, they will destroy the world around you. If they are too cold, they will be ineffective. But if they are warm, your words can bring life, comfort and healing to others.

I cannot count the number of times that I have needed to seek heaven for the right words to say. In my marriage, for example, my constant prayer has to be, "Set a guard, O LORD, over my mouth; keep watch over the door of my lips!" (Psalm 141:3). I have found that relationships are like an obstacle course you can only be successful in if you use the right words. "If anyone thinks he is religious and does not bridle his tongue but deceives his heart, this person's religion is worthless" (James 1:26).

What happens when you do not know what to say? Or what do you do when your feelings and emotions want you to blurt out things that are negative or contrary to God's Word? I pray in the Spirit. Praying in the Spirit means speaking in tongues. "For one who speaks in a tongue speaks not to men but to God; for no one understands him, but he utters mysteries in the Spirit" (1 Corinthians 14:2). This kind of prayer is powered by the Holy Spirit, and I like to believe it means that the enemy cannot understand what I am praying to God.

I did not always want to pray in the Spirit. In fact, I fought the idea of speaking in a heavenly language. One day my pastor was praying over me about speaking in tongues. I rejected his prayer and left. Later, I got on my knees to talk to God. He told me, *You will need to speak in tongues in the circumstances in which I am going to lead you—as a wife, a mother and My follower.*

At that moment I surrendered to it. There was no way I was going to limit God in my life after having seen how He saved me from myself. You must challenge yourself to speak life and God's words daily, because it affects your spiritual life. Jesus warned, "I tell you, on the day of judgment people will give account for every careless word they speak, for by your words you will be justified, and by your words you will be condemned" (Matthew 12:36–37). When you do not have the words to say and the world bogs you down, you can tap into the incredible resource you have of allowing the Holy Spirit to pray through you in your heavenly language.

Touch

Lastly, I want to talk about the spiritual sense of touch. People do not often realize the importance of touch until they cannot touch the ones they love. Leave it to a global pandemic to teach you that. I went months without touching my elderly grandparents during the COVID-19 outbreak. Every time I saw them but could not express my love through physical touch, I felt as if a part of me was being ripped apart. I felt how a newborn baby must feel after he or she is separated from his or her mama right after delivery. Skin-to-skin contact is important to help the precious bundle of joy feel comfort and as if it belongs.

You may have heard the saying that Christians should be the hands and feet of Jesus. That means that we should use our hands and feet to serve others. I cannot tell you how many times I have done things for people reluctantly; however, after I served them, I knew God had been working through me to minister to them. And if you ask someone to pray for you, it feels more effective if the person grabs your hands and prays than if he or she just tells you they prayed for you.

When Jesus walked the earth, He modeled the power of touch. He touched others and healed them, and others touched Him and were healed. We hear about the woman with the issue of blood who touched the hem of Jesus' garment and was made whole (see Matthew 9:20–22; Mark 5:25–34; Luke 8:43–48), but Luke tells us how more than one person was healed that way. "And all the crowd sought to touch him, for power came out from him and healed them all" (Luke 6:19). When tapping into your own spiritual capabilities in Christ, I believe it is possible for all of us to ask God to move through us and provide healing for someone else.

At the same time, there have been instances where I linked arms with people who were not of God, and I felt spiritual oppression because of that connection. When God spoke to Adam and Eve in the garden, He warned them not to touch the forbidden fruit lest they die (see Genesis 3:3). When the apostle Paul recounts the instructions of God, he makes it clear that God does not want His people touching things that are not sanctified before Him.

> "'I will make my dwelling among them and walk among them, and I will be their God, and they shall be my people. Therefore go out from their midst, and be separate from them,' says the Lord, 'and touch no unclean thing; then I will welcome you, and I will be a father to you, and you shall be sons and daughters to me,' says the Lord Almighty."
>
> 2 Corinthians 6:16–18

You must be sensitive to how God is leading. If you do not use the sense of touch carefully, you can find yourself dealing with unnecessary spiritual opposition.

Discern the Times

As times get darker and we start to live out what we see in the Bible concerning the end times, we need to know how to respond. If you hear of wars, natural disasters, pestilence and famines (see Matthew 24), will you be dumbfounded and wonder what is happening, or will you know how to respond based off of how God leads you in the spiritual realm? How can we know how to respond?

We have to make sure we are hearing, seeing and experiencing the pure presence of God and not any other spirit.

Repent, turn from idolatry, remove distractions, devote your time to God, spend time in His presence, look to Him, read His instructions, listen to His voice, speak His truths over your life and share His love and hope with the world. If you do these things, there is no way you can miss the will of God or be led astray by the evil one. I will close with these thoughts from the apostle Paul.

> I appeal to you therefore, brothers [and sisters], by the mercies of God, to present your bodies as a living sacrifice, holy and acceptable to God, which is your spiritual worship. Do not be conformed to this world, but be transformed by the renewal of your mind, that by testing you may discern what is the will of God, what is good and acceptable and perfect.
>
> Romans 12:1–2

What Do I See?

1. Do you discern spiritually what is happening when you feel as if life is going crazy?
2. What are some moments in your life when you think you missed what God was saying?
3. Can you recall the moments in your life when you heard from God and His voice helped you avoid something bad?
4. What are some of the spiritual senses in which you would like to improve?
5. From this moment on, how will you resist the enemy and his deception?

6. How will you position yourself in the future to be able to discern what is happening in the spiritual realm?

What Can I Learn?

- There is a spiritual realm that dictates what takes place in the natural realm.
- God and the enemy offer different instructions. Listen for God's leading.
- When you are unclear about what God is saying or doing, continue to trust in Him and look to Him. He will protect you.
- Your natural senses can be used to discern what is happening in the spiritual realm.
- Your mind can be a vital part of your discernment.
- Keep your eyes, ears, mouth, thoughts and actions centered on God.

Scriptures for Meditation

Romans 8:5–6

For those who live according to the flesh set their minds on the things of the flesh, but those who live according to the Spirit set their minds on the things of the Spirit. For to set the mind on the flesh is death, but to set the mind on the Spirit is life and peace.

Romans 12:1–2

I appeal to you therefore, brothers [and sisters], by the mercies of God, to present your bodies as a living sacrifice, holy and acceptable to God, which is your spiritual worship. Do not be conformed to this world, but be transformed by the renewal of your mind, that by testing you may discern what is the will of God, what is good and acceptable and perfect.

1 Corinthians 2:11–16

No one comprehends the thoughts of God except the Spirit of God. Now we have received not the spirit of the world, but the Spirit who is from God, that we might understand the things freely given us by God. And we impart this in words not taught by human wisdom but taught by the Spirit, interpreting spiritual truths to those who are spiritual. The natural person does not accept the things of the Spirit of God, for they are folly to him, and he is not able to understand them because they are spiritually discerned. The spiritual person judges all things, but is himself to be judged by no one. "For who has understood the mind of the Lord so as to instruct him?" But we have the mind of Christ.

Prayer and Declaration

Father God, thank You for all of the wisdom that You give to us in Your Word. Help me to keep my spiritual senses sharp. May my thoughts be set on You, my eyes look to You, my ears be inclined to Your instructions, my mouth speak words of life and wisdom and my hands and feet bring comfort and help to others. Lord, I pray that You would keep my spiritual discernment accurate. I resist the enemy and his lies, and I press into You. Help me to continue to seek guidance from You to know what You are doing in my life and the world around me. I surrender my life, my heart, my thoughts, my plans to You, God. Have Your way in my life, help me to continually be spiritually sensitive to Your leading, and help me to always respond to Your invitation. Place a shield of protection around me from the attacks of the evil one. My life is Yours. My heart is Yours. Jesus, You alone are the Lord of my life. In Jesus' mighty name, Amen.

ACKNOWLEDGMENTS

This book would not have been possible had it not been for the guidance and encouragement I received from God. Each chapter was written with the leadership of the Holy Spirit, and I am brought to tears just thinking of His faithfulness. To my parents, thank you for allowing me to share my life truthfully and so transparently. Your support has meant everything to me, and I pray that these testimonies will help many come to the hope we have in Christ Jesus. Reverend Renn Law, my hubby and life partner in Christ, thank you for covering me and lifting me up every step of the way. Your love and support made way for my vulnerability and healing. Zion and Teddy (my furbabies), I am so grateful to God for you.

Father Vincenzo Ronchi, Pastor Bill Wilson, Pastor Brian Pettrey, Darryl and Tracy Strawberry and Pastor William McDowell—thank you all for being true reflections of Christ throughout my life. Joe Battaglia, Shari Rigby, Susan Niles and David Sluka, you were each very instrumental in making this possible and helping me trust God for the birth of this book. Your prayers, words and pep talks kept me going. Chosen Books, thank you for believing in me. Lori Janke, my editor, thank you for cleaning me up and keeping my voice as the heartbeat of the stories and teachings shared.

My intercessors: Bri (Sissy), this is all standing on the foundation of those 5 a.m. prayers. J.T. (broty), thank you for always having my back. Mark "The Shark," it was your prophetic vision that helped me get over the roadblocks. Thank you for your prayers. Christine Mantlo and my Purity Girls, throughout my life, there have been many people who have said I should write a book. I thank you, especially, because you spoke all of this before it even happened.

My Most High King Ministries family, my Purity Girls and my spiritual children, this book is dedicated to you! Your willingness to allow me to do life with you and your transparency helped shape the content shared in this book. May this be a testament that you, too, can do all things through Christ who gives us strength!

Jeannie Ortega Law is a singer, speaker, author and actress from New York City who signed her first major record deal with Hollywood Records at the age of sixteen. Ortega Law spent several years on the pop radio circuit. Her first single, "Crowded," yielded a Top 25 slot on the Billboard Hot 100 charts and was certified Gold on radio airplay. Her album *No Place Like Brooklyn* (2006) debuted No. 1 on Billboard's Heatseekers chart. She spent the summer of 2006 as the sole opening act for international pop star Rihanna on her nationwide tour.

In 2007, Ortega Law had a life-changing divine encounter and decided to change direction and use her gifts for God. The multiple-threat performer has been featured several times on the international network TBN. She continues to tour Christian venues and churches throughout the United States as a speaker, sharing her music and communicating her life-changing story. Ortega Law now has a worldwide ministry, Most High King Ministries, with her husband, Reverend Renn Law, and she continues to make music from an inspirational perspective. Her on-screen appearances include *One Life to Live, Step Up* and more. Ortega Law has her own TV show, *In the Mix*, on 24 Flix. She is widely known as a worship leader, media personality and Christian journalist.

www.ingramcontent.com/pod-product-compliance
Lightning Source LLC
Chambersburg PA
CBHW060653150426
42813CB00053B/795